creative·stamping

with mixed media techniques

sherrill kahn

NORTH LIGHT BOOKS

North Light Books
Cincinnati, Ohio
www.artistsnetwork.com

DEDICATION

I want to dedicate this book to my wonderful, caring and supportive **husband, Joel**. *He constantly inspires and encourages me. He often accompanies me on my many teaching trips and shows incredible patience when we have to change our plans so that I can meet my deadlines or get ready to go off and teach again.*

He is my best friend and mentor.

Other fine North Light Books are available from your local bookstore, art supply store or direct from the publisher.

07 06 05 04 03   5 4 3 2 1

Library of Congress Cataloging-in-Publication Data

Kahn, Sherrill
    Creative stamping with mixed media techniques / by Sherrill Kahn.
        p. cm.
    ISBN 1-58180-347-8 (alk. paper)
    1. Rubber stamp printing. 2. Mixed media painting—Technique. 3. Decoration and ornament. I. Title.

    TT867.K34 2003
    761—dc21

                                          2002045508

EDITOR: Liz Koffel Schneiders
DESIGNER: Andrea Short
LAYOUT ARTIST: Karla Baker
PRODUCTION COORDINATOR: Michelle Ruberg
PHOTOGRAPHERS: Christine Polomsky and Tim Grondin
PHOTO STYLIST: Kim Brown

METRIC CONVERSION CHART

TO CONVERT	TO	MULTIPLY BY
Inches	Centimeters	2.54
Centimeters	Inches	0.4
Feet	Centimeters	30.5
Centimeters	Feet	0.03
Yards	Meters	0.9
Meters	Yards	1.1
Sq. Inches	Sq. Centimeters	6.45
Sq. Centimeters	Sq. Inches	0.16
Sq. Feet	Sq. Meters	0.09
Sq. Meters	Sq. Feet	10.8
Sq. Yards	Sq. Meters	0.8
Sq. Meters	Sq. Yards	1.2
Pounds	Kilograms	0.45
Kilograms	Pounds	2.2
Ounces	Grams	28.4
Grams	Ounces	0.04

ABOUT THE AUTHOR

Artist **Sherrill Kahn** *has been creating award-winning drawings, paintings and fiber artwork for almost forty years. She enjoys experimenting with a variety of different media and lives by the words "What if?"*

Sherrill taught for thirty years in the Los Angeles Public Schools. Currently, she teaches workshops across the country, where she loves sharing her innovative and fun rubber-stamping and mixed media techniques with others.

Sherrill's work can be found in private collections worldwide. Her work has appeared in Somerset Studio, Expression, Belle Armoire, Quilting Arts *and other magazines related to fiber arts and rubber stamping. She is the author of* Creating With Paint, New Ways, New Materials. *She also has a fabric line from Robert Kaufman showing some of her painting styles, and many of her stamp patterns are available as Rollagraph stamp wheels from Clearsnap.*

Sherrill lives in Encino, California, with her husband, Joel. They own and operate the rubber stamp company "Impress Me." Visit their Web site at **www.impressmenow.com.**

THANK YOU'S

I want to **thank** *my editor, Liz Schneiders, and my photographer, Christine Polomsky. Their incredible ideas have contributed greatly to this book.*

I want to thank all of my many students who have inspired and encouraged me. Thank you so much.

I want to thank all of the teachers who helped me develop the techniques that I use constantly in my work. Without all of you, I could never do what I do.

I want to thank my sister, Anjani, for protecting and encouraging me since I was a little girl. Thank you, sis.

Finally, I want to thank all of my friends who have always been there for me. **You enrich my life.**

TABLE OF CONTENTS

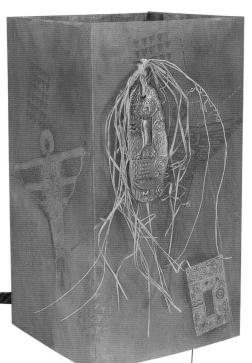

I saw the angel in the

marble and carved until I

set him free.

.

Michelangelo

Imagination...its limits

are only those of the

mind itself.

Rod Serling

INTRODUCTION

i am excited about sharing the mixed media and stamping techniques in this book with all of you. So many of you want to know how I create the layered look that gives my creative projects pizzazz. It is my hope that this book will help demystify that process and that you'll have lots of fun along the way.

People often ask me, "Where do you get your ideas?" It is an easy question to answer. I constantly ask myself, "what if?" I try new things—some ideas work great and others don't work at all. Often the pieces that don't work lead me in a different path that does work. I also teach a wonderful group of stimulating students and am inspired by their ideas. Look at this book as an invitation to experiment with a whole new array of stamping techniques. Hopefully you will find inspiration as I did to take your creativity in a new direction.

Do not be afraid of the blank pieces of paper or fabric that sit on the surface in front of you. Tell yourself, "It is only a piece of paper." If you do, you will be free to explore all of the creative possibilities. You will always learn something while involved in the creative process. You might learn that the surface was too wet, or that you don't like that color combination or the way the paints worked together. When you do the next project, that information will influence what you do.

Keep a **spirit of play and exploration** and you will have a wonderful time making your beautiful creations.

HOW TO USE THIS BOOK

t his book is divided into two main sections. In the first half, I'll share over a dozen step-by-step sequences on paper and fabric that combine some of my favorite mixed media techniques. The purpose of these "recipes" is to give you a chance to practice layering and combining techniques for a dramatic and colorful surface. I have included a number of new techniques in this section, along with tips on how to use glazing in your projects. Just the simple process of glazing a color over the surface will change the look of the piece completely.

The second half of the book presents twelve craft projects. Each project highlights a different set of techniques and shows you how to decorate and embellish any surface from wood to silk to terra cotta. There are also techniques for adding fun embellishments to your projects, such as beads made out of air-dry clay, Tyvek and shrink plastic.

This book is very experimental. I thought of the words "play" and "what if" while I did each piece. Follow the recipes and projects in this book, and then go and experiment on your own. Constantly push the envelope. Try painting with colors that you don't usually use or surfaces that have interested you. Embellish your work with every imaginable item, such as beads, buttons, collage, yarn, ribbons or any other creative item you wish to use. If you get stuck, refer to the sections on adding pizzazz or embellishments to your work. Play every day and, above all, have fun!

Tools & Materials

rubber stamping can be combined with dozens of different paints, surfaces and embellishments. There is always some new tool or material to try. This section introduces you to the tools and materials I used when creating the projects and designs found in this book.

>>>>> CHOOSING & PREPARING SURFACES

Almost any surface can be painted, rubber stamped and embellished. The projects in this book will give you a chance to try out all of the surfaces listed here. I would encourage you to try other surfaces as well. Experiment to find out how each surface responds and keep notes on your experiments so that you know what works best.

HEAT SET YOUR PAINTED FABRIC

After using paint on fabric, it must be heat set. This will fix the paint on the fabric so that you can wash the fabric without altering the design.

Place your painted piece of fabric face down on top of a water-resistant paper, such as deli paper, placed on an ironing board. Press the fabric for a minute or two using the temperature setting appropriate for the fabric you are ironing. You may use steam if you wish. Iron the back of the fabric first and then the front of the fabric.

PAPER: Paper is a logical choice for painting and rubber stamping. Choose heavier rather than lighter papers if you are mixing water with your paint. Cardstock is good for most projects, but watercolor paper is wonderful for wet techniques because it is less likely to buckle. If you are stamping detailed images, choose a smooth paper.

FABRIC: Most fabrics can be rubber stamped and painted. Each fabric type accepts paint differently, so practice on a sample swatch to see how well it works. For the demonstrations in this book, I used Robert Kaufman's Pima and Kona cottons, available at most fabric stores. Any tightly woven fabric with a high thread count will work. Silk is another excellent fabric. Jacquard's Dye-Na-Flow is magnificent on silk.

Do not prewash your fabric. Prewashed fabric is more absorbent and sometimes doesn't give stamped impressions that are crisp and clean.

WOOD: Wood can be easily rubber stamped and accepts most paints. Seal it with wood primer and sand any rough spots before painting. Most wood items purchased in craft stores come presanded.

Once you are done painting your project, you may want to apply a clear coat of varnish to protect your painted surface. This is especially helpful on items such as wooden trays, which may occasionally get wet. If your completed project has any unpainted surfaces, such as the back of a piece of wood used to mount a tile, apply a coat of wood primer so the wood will not warp.

VELLUM: Translucent papers such as vellum make wonderful surfaces for stamping. I use a stiff, noncurling vellum called Sheer Heaven for all of my stamping projects. It is superb for all painting and drawing techniques, including wet techniques. Turn to the Resources on page 126 to find Sheer Heaven in a luminaria kit for painting.

PAPIER MÂCHÉ: Papier mâché boxes and frames readily accept most painting and rubber stamping techniques. They are inexpensive, lightweight and require no priming or sanding.

TERRA COTTA: Flowerpots and other unglazed ceramics make fun stamping surfaces. For the curved sides of a pot, I like to apply acrylic paint with sponges or unmounted rubber stamps.

AIR-DRY CLAY: Air-dry clay is sold in packages in craft stores. Great for making beads, it can be impressed with rubber stamps and painted with acrylic-based paint. Unlike polymer clay, it needs no baking and dries quickly. I use Das air-dry clay, which comes in both white and terra cotta.

SHRINK PLASTIC: Shrink plastic is a thin, flexible plastic that thickens and shrinks when heated. Shrink plastic makes beautiful beads and charms for embellishing all kinds of craft projects. Color it and stamp it either before or after shrinking. I use PolyShrink shrink plastic from Lucky Squirrel.

TYVEK: Tyvek is a strong, flexible sheet of spun plastic fibers used to make envelopes. While it looks like paper, it cannot be torn and it shrinks when heated with a heat gun. It makes a wonderful surface to color, shrink and stamp. It can be made into textured beads. You can buy Tyvek envelopes in office supply stores.

Use a face mask or work in a well-ventilated area when heating Tyvek to protect against potentially toxic fumes.

>>>>> EMBELLISHMENTS

BEADS: I often use seed beads to embellish fabric projects. I also string seed beads onto wire when creating wire beads. Larger beads can be used as decorative accents.

RAFFIA: Raffia is a wonderful embellishment for three-dimensional projects and books. Rayon raffia is shiny and feels like plastic and comes in many colors. Natural and rayon raffia are available in craft stores and some stationery stores.

EMBOSSING POWDERS: Embossing powders create a raised image when dusted over wet pigment ink and heated with a heat gun. Embossing powders come in all colors and range from very fine to thick powders. I like to use embossing powders from Ranger.

THREAD AND CORD: Waxed polyester thread is available in a variety of colors and weights. It is stronger and heavier than most threads and can be found in bead, craft and rubber stamp stores. I use the thread for binding books and making jewelry, and for adding dangles to creative projects. Heavier cord is good for making necklaces.

tools & • materials

>>>>> PAINTS & INKS

Walking through any art or rubber stamp store will yield an amazing variety of paints and inks. The key to using any colorant is to experiment and find out how each colorant will react with other colorants and to different surfaces. Some paints and dyes work better on paper, others on fabric. Some are translucent while others are very opaque. I constantly experiment with each product to discover its potential. New products come out daily and each will have its own special properties.

ACRYLIC PAINTS: There are a variety of acrylic paints available. There are tube acrylics, jar acrylics and bottled acrylics. Acrylics are ideal for use on wood, paper and unglazed ceramics. Always buy the best acrylics you can afford. Look for highly pigmented acrylics that will remain vibrant even when diluted with water. I recommend Golden's tube acrylics.

Two of my favorite jar acrylics are Neopaque and Sherrill's Sorbets by Jacquard. Both are opaque, highly pigmented and light-bodied. They do not dry stiff on fabric and they work beautifully on other surfaces. Neopaque comes in a rich range of decorator colors with a slight mica shimmer, while Sherrill's Sorbets are soft matte pastels. Both rubber stamp beautifully and show up brilliantly on dark surfaces.

PIGMENT-BASED FABRIC DYES:
Pigment-based fabric dye is a free-flowing acrylic-based paint similar to dye. I recommend Jacquard's Dye-Na-Flow. This paint works beautifully on fabric, especially on silk, and also on paper and cardboard. When dry, the paint is waterproof, although it must be heat set to be permanent on fabric. It is similar to liquid watercolors when applied to paper. Mix Dye-Na-Flow with Lumiere in a small cup to make interesting metallic washes.

METALLIC AND PEARLESCENT PAINTS: Acrylics with metallic or pearlescent highlights are available in art, craft or rubber stamping stores in a variety of colors. I recommend Lumiere, a light-bodied acrylic with great coverage ability. The light-reflecting abilities of this paint are dazzling. It is excellent for stamping or sponging metallic highlights.

TEXTILE PAINT: Textile Color by Jacquard is incredibly versatile. It is a thick, transparent colored paint. Its transparency makes it perfect for creating rich and exciting glazes when sponged or brushed over other colors on fabric or paper. I used Textile Colors in many of the projects in this book.

DYE RE-INKERS: Dye re-inkers are squeeze bottles of dye ink used to reapply ink to a dye ink pad. Look for dye re-inkers with ink that is permanent on most surfaces. Use the ink on an ink pad or squeeze it directly onto a brush or sponge. My favorite brand is Clearsnap's Ancient Page re-inkers. The colors are rich and vibrant. I have used them on everything from paper to fabric with stunning results.

WATER-SOLUBLE CRAYONS: These crayons create delicate watercolor washes when wet with a damp brush or sponge.

>>>>> STAMPING TOOLS

The projects in this book use rubber stamps, but also explore techniques that use several nontraditional tools. It is fun to try alternative tools in addition to traditional rubber stamps. Experiment with all of these tools and then combine your favorite techniques for even more impressive results. Don't forget to take notes on your experiments. These notes will become a handy reference tool later on.

RUBBER STAMPS: All projects in this book were stamped using rubber stamps that I personally designed and sell through my mail-order stamp company, "Impress Me." "Impress Me" is an angel company, which means that if you make hand-stamped cards or gifts with these stamps, you have permission to sell the projects at craft shows. The rubber stamps are unmounted, so they are well suited for stamping curved surfaces. They are also easy to clean.

UNINKED STAMP PADS: You can create custom stamp pads by squeezing paint directly onto an uninked stamp pad. Pat rubber stamps on the pad or roll a Rollagraph stamp wheel through the paint. You can also mix more than one color of paint on an uninked pad. I like to use Clearsnap's uninked stamp pads.

MOLDABLE FOAM TIPS AND STYLUS: Colorbox creates a clever stylus with moldable foam tips in a variety of shapes and sizes. Heat the moldable foam with a lightbulb or heat gun and press it into a textured surface such as a button, window screen or rubber stamp to create your own custom foam stamp. If you don't like the first impression, you can reheat it and create a new impression. Let your imagination be your guide. For larger images, try using Penscore, a large, soft foam block that can be heated and textured to form a small print plate.

ROLLAGRAPHS: A Rollagraph is a continuous wheel-shaped rubber stamp attached to a Rollagraph handle. A Rollagraph lets you stamp long strips of repetitive patterns very quickly and easily. You can purchase Rollagraphs with special ink cartridges that attach to the handle. I prefer to roll them through ink on traditional stamp pads or through paint applied to uninked pads or a large hydrophilic sponge.

EXTRA-THICK CRAFT FOAM: Large, thick craft foam sheets can be used as printing plates. I recommend Ranger's Cut n' Dry Foam. Cut n' Dry Foam can also be textured by heating and stamping its foam surface, similar to Penscore.

RUBBER BANDS: Any thick surface can be wrapped with crisscrossed rubber bands to make a print plate. I use corrugated cardboard, thick foam and foam core board for making print plates. Choose rubber bands of varying widths and thicknesses to get different results. See page 19 to learn how to make a rubber band print plate.

FOAM TAKE-OUT CONTAINERS: Wonderful handmade stamps can be made with foam take-out lids, meat trays and plates. Trim the excess from the foam container with a sharp pair of scissors. Draw your design onto the foam with a ballpoint pen and then sponge paint onto the finished print plate. Press the painted plate onto the chosen surface. See page 18 to learn how to use a foam print plate.

tools & · materials

>>>>> GENERAL CRAFT TOOLS

AWL: Use a heavy awl when punching holes into thick surfaces such as papier mâché boxes or journal covers. It makes it easy to attach embellishments such as raffia, charms and buttons.

BONE FOLDER: Bone folders are essential for making books. They are used to make sharp creases on the covers and pages of the book.

BRAYER: I use a brayer to roll out clay for stamping clay beads and for rolling over glued pieces to be sure they stick flat. Brayers can also be used to apply paint to a chosen surface.

CRAFT KNIFE AND CUTTING MAT: Use a sharp craft knife when cutting thick board or cardstock. The knives can also be used for cutting pages and handmade stencils. When using craft knives for cutting, place a self-healing mat under the surface being cut and be sure that your ruler has a metal edge.

DELI PAPER: To protect my work surface, I place deli paper or other water-resistant paper under my projects. I prefer sheets of white, unfolded deli paper. The advantage to using deli paper is that in addition to protecting your work surface, it accepts most paints and rubber stamping beautifully. It is also great for collage. Deli paper is also handy for placing under fabric when you heat set it. You can find deli paper at restaurant supply stores and large discount warehouse clubs.

FABRIC GLUE: When working on fabric, use fabric glue instead of ordinary white craft glue. It is waterproof when dry, so projects can be washed if necessary. Fabric glue works beautifully for all fabric gluing situations.

FINE MIST SPRAY BOTTLE: I use a spray bottle filled with water when wetting a paper or fabric for wet-into-wet techniques.

HEAVY-DUTY WHITE CRAFT GLUE: A strong, extra-thick craft glue is best for any difficult gluing projects. My favorite heavy-duty white glue is The Ultimate from Crafter's Pick.

HOLE PUNCHES: Use $\frac{1}{16}$" (1.5mm) punches for making small holes in embellishments. Use $\frac{1}{8}$" (3mm) punches when making holes in shrink plastic. Decorative hole punches make wonderful designs on paper or cardstock.

KNITTING NEEDLE: I use metal knitting needles to hold projects in place that will be heated. I wrap the blunt end of the needle with sponge squares and duct tape so that it remains cool when I am heating shrink plastic or Tyvek.

NEEDLE TOOL: Use a needle tool for making holes in polymer and air-dry clay, paper and cardstock.

PAPER ADHESIVE: Some glues work better on paper than others. I recommend clear-drying glues that are non-toxic and archival, and clean up with water after drying. Memory Mount by Crafter's Pick is excellent for gluing paper together. If you are working on very small projects, a glue stick is also a good choice.

SCISSORS: Have sharp paper and fabric scissors on hand when working on creative projects.

STAPLER: Use a standard stapler when making small stapled books. Use a heavy-duty, deep throat stapler for making larger stapled books.

STEEL-EDGED RULER: Steel-edged rulers are easier to use than plastic rulers. Plastic rulers can be scarred by cutting tools, damaging them for future use.

>>>>> TOOLS FOR DAZZLING EFFECTS

Ordinary craft items and household tools can be used for some great special effects. This list covers the items I use most often to add something extra to my work.

APPLICATOR-TIPPED BOTTLES: Paint or ink applied directly with a squeeze bottle and fine applicator tip creates wonderful designs. You can purchase Jacquard paints prepackaged in squeeze bottles and simply attach a metal applicator tip, or you can buy their empty squeeze bottles and fill them with your own paint. You can find small squeeze bottles with 5mm, 7mm and 9mm metal tips in craft and rubber stamp stores. I prefer the 7mm tip.

The bottles can be filled using a Monoject 412 extruder (a large, plastic syringe) available from medical suppliers and some craft stores.

BLEACH: Bleach can be applied to sponges and patted onto rubber stamps for bleached impressions on dark, acid-free surfaces. Use bleach with extreme caution as it is very toxic. I use the bleach full strength, but it can be diluted slightly with water for different effects. Choose 100 percent cotton and acid-free paper when doing bleach techniques.

BATTERY-OPERATED TOOTHBRUSH: A battery-operated toothbrush is a versatile craft tool. Use one to apply paint through a screen or stencil onto your surface. It also creates interesting textures in wet paint already on the surface. A battery-operated toothbrush is great for cleaning paint off of rubber stamps and your hands.

BRUSHES: I experiment with many inexpensive acrylic brushes. I prefer using a variety of flat brushes and detail brushes, which are helpful for painting highlights in small areas.

CREDIT CARD OR PAINT SCRAPER: I use old credit cards or a variety of paint scrapers to apply paint and texture to creative projects. They are also great for spreading an even layer of glue over a large area.

HEAT GUN (EMBOSSING GUN): A heat gun is a versatile tool. It is great for embossing and working with shrink plastic and moldable craft foam. Use one to dry your fabric or paper when you're in a hurry. For shrink plastic work, choose a heat gun with a large opening. I prefer Ranger's Heatit Craft Tool. Most other heat guns have small openings that may not work as well with shrink plastic.

MASKING TAPE: Masking tape makes an excellent block for painted and stamped impressions. If you are working on fabric, regular masking tape can be used. Choose a low-tack or specialty masking tape on paper to keep the tape from tearing the paper.

MOLDING PASTE: Stamp into molding paste to add texture to any surface. The paste is thick and accepts incredible impressions with rubber stamps. Paint the surface with dry-brushing techniques after the paste has dried. Golden makes a variety of quality molding pastes.

SALT: Salt creates dramatic and beautiful patterns when sprinkled into wet paint and left to dry. There are a variety of salts available and each gives different results on wet surfaces. You can use rock salt, kosher salt, ice cream salt, table salt or any other salt you can find. Try each salt and take notes on the results. I use Jacquard Silk Salt for most of my salt projects.

SPONGES: Sponges are the most important tools that I use. They are used for applying paint to stamps and to the chosen surface. Use "hydrophilic" sponges, which do not dry stiff after wetting but remain pliable and soft. I prefer the sponge that is golden yellow in color with rounded edges. It is commonly found in paint, wallpaper and tile departments of large home improvement warehouses. Use a sharp pair of scissors to cut the sponges into squares varying in size from 1" to 2" (2.5cm to 5cm). You can also use textural sponges to add interest to your creative projects. An uncut sponge makes a good stamp pad.

Getting Started

i know you are excited about starting the projects and mixed media recipes in this book. Nevertheless, take a moment to review the tips and suggestions mentioned here. Having an organized work space will make the creative process easier and more enjoyable, so I've noted some helpful tips below. The facing page offers the most basic techniques I use for applying paint to my pieces. You might find an approach here that is new to you.

>>>> ORGANIZING YOUR WORK SPACE

It is easier to create if your work space is organized. Place similar supplies, such as brushes, markers, different types of paint and stamp pads, together in plastic or wire containers so that they are easily moved to where you need them. Have a stack of paper towels and clean water available to rinse off brushes and unmounted rubber stamps as you work. Change your water frequently so that the colors remain clean. When cleaning rubber stamps, try using a battery-operated toothbrush.

Working with paint can be messy. Be sure to wear an apron or old clothes while you work. Protect your work surface with sheets of water-resistant paper such as freezer or deli paper. Before you go to bed, straighten up your work space so it is ready when you begin work again. No matter how large your work area is, organization is necessary to use the area efficiently.

WORK SPACE TIP:
CREATING "SERENDIPITY" FABRIC OR PAPER

When working on a painted sample, I always end up with leftover paint on my brushes, sponges and rubber stamps. To keep this wonderful paint from going to waste, I have a stack of blank scraps of fabric or cardstock next to me at all times. As I work on my project, I clean my sponge, rubber stamp or brush on these scraps. When one serendipity piece gets full of paint, I start on another. Over time, I have a stack of colorful scraps ready to use in other creative projects. See pages 104–107 for a fun project using serendipity fabric.

>>>>> WORKING WITH PAINT

The following basic techniques are helpful if you are just getting started with stamping in mixed media. Perhaps you have been stamping for a long time but are accustomed to only using rubber stamps and dye and pigment ink pads in your stamping projects. The following techniques should inspire you to look at your tools in a whole new way. Follow these tips when applying paint with a sponge, a Rollagraph, a stamp or an applicator tip.

APPLYING PAINT WITH A SPONGE

One of the easiest ways to apply paint directly onto a surface is with a sponge. Squeeze one or more colors of paint directly onto the sponge and stamp the surface. If the sponge runs low on paint, add more paint or lightly spritz the sponge with water to extract the most pigment.

INKING A ROLLAGRAPH STAMP

Uninked stamp pads or large hydrophilic sponges give you the flexibility to use a variety of nontraditional paints and inks with your rubber stamps. Simply apply paint to the stamp pad or sponge with a squeeze bottle or spoon and spread the paint evenly on the surface. Roll the stamp pattern of the Rollagraph through the paint repeatedly until the paint covers the entire surface of the Rollagraph.

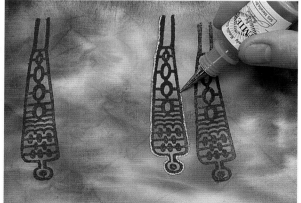

APPLYING PAINT TO A RUBBER STAMP

You can apply paint directly onto the surface of a rubber stamp with a sponge. For softly blended colors, sponge different colors of paint onto different parts of the stamp.

APPLYING PAINT WITH A METAL APPLICATOR TIP

Attach a 7mm metal applicator tip to the top of any fine-tipped squeeze bottle of acrylic paint. The metal tip allows you to draw beautiful fine lines and dots.

Creating Stamped Backgrounds

a n interesting background serves as the foundation for beautiful artwork. One of the easiest ways to create an effective background is through repetition. Stamped images, when repeated, can create simple yet rich backgrounds full of texture. They are easy to do and create wonderful patterns perfect for applying to many surfaces. This section will teach you a few stamping techniques that demonstrate a number of different ways to create interesting backgrounds with rubber stamps, sponges, and print plates made from foam plates or cardboard wrapped with rubber bands.

>>>>> STAMPING BACKGROUNDS WITH PERMANENT INKS

When working on cardstock or other smooth surface, choose a permanent dye ink for stamping. Later, if you choose to add another layer of color on top, the stamped impressions won't bleed or run. In this demonstration, I used a shell pattern with four images in a square. You can substitute any stamp as long as you can place the images close together on the paper.

1 INK THE STAMP

Pat the ink pad onto the surface of your rubber stamp. I am using an unmounted rubber stamp for this technique.

2 STAMP THE CARDSTOCK

Stamp the cardstock, starting at the edge of the paper.

3 COVER THE ENTIRE SURFACE

Continue stamping until you have covered the entire surface with patterns, leaving no gaps in the design.

>>>>> STAMPING WITH BLEACH

Bleach will leave a subtle and beautiful impression when stamped onto dark, acid-free paper and dark natural fabrics such as cotton. You can use either a rubber stamp or sponge for this technique. When using liquid bleach, be very careful and have good ventilation. Children should only do this technique supervised by an adult.

1 TEST YOUR SURFACE

Dip an acrylic brush into the bleach and paint a small square on the edge of the surface to test how well it reacts to the bleach.

2 APPLY BLEACH TO THE STAMP

Dip a sponge square into the bleach and pat the bleach onto the rubber stamp.

3 STAMP THE SURFACE

Stamp the paper with the bleach. Continue stamping the image until you have the entire surface covered.

>>>>> STAMPING WITH A SPONGE

A soft square sponge makes an ideal stamping tool. You can create any pattern you choose depending on how you apply the paint. Black fabric and cardstock are highly effective surfaces to use when creating this kind of background. Metallic paints such as Lumiere are especially gorgeous when applied to a dark surface.

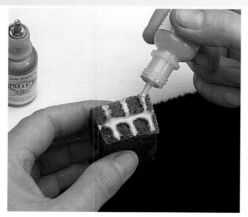

1 SQUEEZE PAINT ONTO A SPONGE

Squeeze a pattern onto the sponge surface with Gold and Bronze Lumiere or other thick metallic acrylic paint.

2 STAMP THE FABRIC

Stamp repeat images on the fabric. If you run out of paint, add more to the sponge. Continue until the pattern covers the surface.

3 ADD A SECOND PATTERN ON TOP

You can further embellish your background by stamping over the first pattern in a contrasting color. I used Copper Lumiere in this example.

creating stamped·backgrounds

>>>> STAMPING WITH A FOAM PRINT PLATE

Foam picnic plates, meat trays or take-out containers can be turned into wonderful print plates with just a pair of scissors and a ballpoint pen. Use a print plate for instant stamped backgrounds on paper or fabric. Any paint or ink can be used for this technique. For an interesting variation, use light-colored, opaque acrylics on black fabric.

1 DRAW A PATTERN ON THE FOAM

To create a foam print plate, cut a foam lid from a take-out container into a rectangular shape. Draw a simple design with a ballpoint pen onto the foam.

2 APPLY INK TO THE PLATE

Pat permanent dye-based ink pads onto the surface of the foam print plate.

3 STAMP THE IMAGE

Print the design several times, adding more ink to the plate as you go. Less ink will leave lighter impressions; more ink will leave heavier impressions.

>>>> STAMPING WITH MOLDABLE FOAM

Clearsnap manufactures a wonderful product called Penscore. When it is heated, you can impress any texture into the surface and create a print plate. If you don't like the result, you can reheat the surface and make another print plate.

1 HEAT THE FOAM SURFACE

Heat a block of Penscore foam with an embossing heat gun.

2 PRESS INTO THE FOAM WITH A STAMP

Use a rubber stamp large enough to cover the entire block and press firmly into the heated foam.

3 STAMP WITH ACRYLIC PAINT

Sponge paint onto the textured surface of the Penscore. Print on either fabric or cardstock.

creating stamped·backgrounds

>>>>> STAMPING WITH A RUBBER BAND PRINT PLATE

If you are accustomed to using rubber stamps, this technique is a great way to broaden your creativity. When working on a dark surface, remember to choose an opaque paint that will be visible when printed. When working on light-colored surfaces, you can also do this technique using transparent fabric dyes and textile paints.

① WRAP THE CARDBOARD WITH RUBBER BANDS

To make a rubber band print plate, stretch several flat rubber bands in a diagonal pattern around a 5" x 7" (12.7cm x 17.8cm) or similarly sized piece of heavy corrugated cardboard.

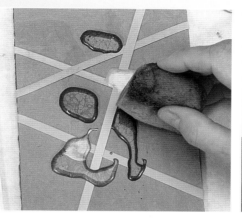

② SQUEEZE PAINT ONTO THE PRINT PLATE

Squeeze acrylic paints in several colors onto the print plate. This sample uses Copper, Bronze, Violet and Blue Lumiere.

③ SPREAD THE PAINT

Sponge the colors across the print plate so they are loosely blended. Use enough paint to keep the surface wet before printing.

④ LAY THE PRINT PLATE ON THE FABRIC

Turn the print plate face down onto the black fabric. Press it firmly in place.

⑤ WORK THE PAINT INTO THE FABRIC

Flip the fabric face up and press over the entire surface with your fingers to work the paint into the fabric.

⑥ LIFT THE FABRIC OFF THE PLATE

Pull the fabric from the plate. To print a second image beside the first, sponge additional colors onto the print plate and print again.

creating stamped·backgrounds

Color Layering Techniques

Layering color is a fun and exciting process. Applying one color over another so that they blend and react with one another is one of the most magical ways to add some pizzazz to your work. There are dozens of ways to layer color, but the two most common techniques that I use are glazing and dry sponging. Once you learn how to use these two techniques well, you can combine them with stamping for many design effects.

>>>>> LAYERING COLOR WITH GLAZING

A glaze is a transparent layer of color that is applied on top of another color so that the two colors interact. The bottom color can be seen through the top color. You can glaze just about any surface. The important thing to remember is to use transparent-colored paints, such as Jacquard's Textile Colors, or washes and fabric dyes, such as Dye-Na-Flow. Opaque paints will cover the underlying color.

➡

THE MAGIC OF GLAZING

Each of these strips of fabric was torn from the same piece of painted cloth. Each was glazed in a different color of Jacquard's Textile Colors. The transparent color of the glaze affected the colors underneath it. Notice how some colors became more intense while others became more muted. A blue glaze over yellow will create a soft green. Glazing is an easy and exciting way to change the mood and personality of a piece.

control
piece

white   goldenrod   scarlet   russet

violet   fluorescent violet   periwinkle   apple green   turquoise

>>>>> GLAZING BACKGROUNDS STEP BY STEP

Transparent Textile Colors make wonderful backgrounds. They are highly pigmented, yet they are transparent. This makes them perfectly suited for glazing techniques. Applying one color over another alters the color below, creating exciting new colors.

 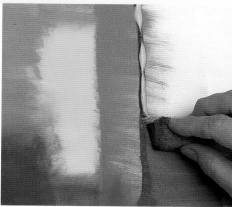 

❶ SPREAD OUT THE FIRST COLOR

With an applicator-tipped bottle, squeeze a line of Goldenrod Textile Color onto white cotton fabric and spread the color across the fabric with a sponge square.

❷ GLAZE WITH ADDITIONAL COLORS

Add additional colors in the same manner. Overlap the edges of each color so that they blend. I used Fluorescent Violet, Scarlet Red, Violet and Periwinkle Textile Colors.

❸ ADD DEPTH WITH MORE GLAZING

Glaze Scarlet Red paint over the Goldenrod in the center of the image. Notice how it creates a soft, rich orange.

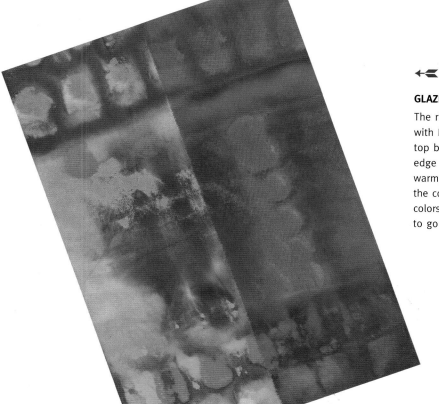

GLAZING ON FABRIC

The right side of this fabric has been glazed with Dye-Na-Flow. The bright yellow spots on top became a subtle green. The bottom edge was glazed in red, giving that section a warm, uniform glow. You can easily control the contrast and the mix of warm and cool colors in a piece by selecting the right glazes to go on top of the lower layers.

color·layering *techniques*

>>>>> LAYERING COLOR WITH DRY SPONGING

Dry sponging is a variation on glazing techniques. The biggest difference is that you layer color by sponging on a light coat of paint with a dry sponge. It is similar to applying blush to your cheeks. The edges are soft and the color has an airbrushed appearance. The advantage of dry sponging is that you can use it to apply a layer of opaque paints such as Neopaque and light-colored acrylics such as Sherrill's Sorbets while still allowing some of the underlying colors to show through.

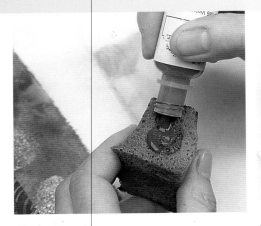  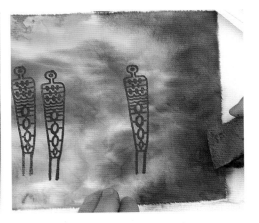

1 SQUEEZE PAINT ONTO A SPONGE

Squeeze Violet Neopaque or some other deep-colored opaque acrylic paint onto a sponge square.

2 WIPE OFF THE EXCESS PAINT TO CREATE A "DRY SPONGE"

Sponge the excess color onto scrap paper so that there is a thin layer of paint still left on the sponge. Check the sponge to make sure there aren't any shiny areas of paint.

3 DRY SPONGE OVER THE EDGES

On a busy and colorful piece, dry sponge the Violet around the edges of the design. Apply just enough paint to deepen the colors without covering them completely.

THE ORIGINAL FABRIC SAMPLE

THE FINISHED PIECE AFTER DRY SPONGING

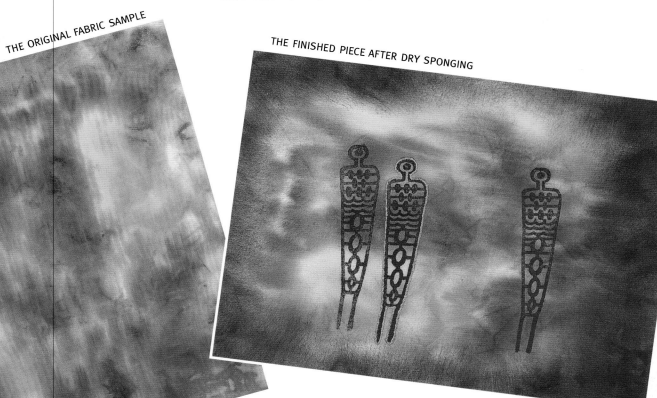

>>>>> COMBINING GLAZING AND DRY SPONGING

You can combine glazing and dry sponging in the same piece. Remember that transparent glazes of Textile Color can be used straight from the bottle, while opaque paints should be applied using a dry-sponging technique.

① BEGIN GLAZING THE SURFACE

For this demonstration, start with the foam print plate made on page 18. To simplify the design, sponge Turquoise Textile Color over the printed design.

② DEEPEN THE GLAZED COLORS

Apply additional Turquoise to unify the design. Since the paint is transparent, it can be applied thick and wet and still allow the underlying colors to show through.

③ DRY SPONGE THE EDGES

After stamping additional pattern onto the surface with a stamp, dry sponge Violet Neopaque on the edges of the design.

The finished Sample

Layers of color create a sense of depth and richness in this piece. Glazing and dry sponging unify the contrasting colors underneath beautifully.

color·layering *techniques*

mixed media ·recipes·

in this section, I want to introduce you to a series of "recipes" in which you will learn how to combine some of the basic stamping and color layering techniques shown earlier. Think of each of these as a mini workshop where you can experiment with new techniques and learn how to use them for the greatest impact.

recipe one:
Making Simple Sponged Patterns

Sponging patterns is easy and lots of fun to do. The pattern possibilities are endless. By adding a layer of highly pigmented fabric dye on top, you create a spectacular piece to use in your creative projects. I usually use Dye-Na-Flow for wet backgrounds and around sponged patterns since the paint flows beautifully around heavier-bodied acrylics.

supplies:

- sponge squares
- Lumiere: Bronze, Gold and Super Sparkle
- two pieces of white cotton fabric with a high thread count
- fine mist spray bottle filled with water
- Dye-Na-Flow: assorted colors
- Neopaque: Violet
- uninked stamp pad
- Rollagraph with wheel stamp

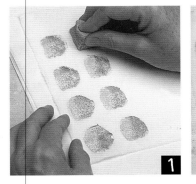
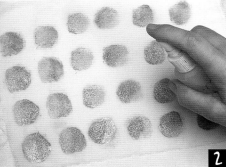

1 SPONGE SPOTS OF LUMIERE

Apply three colors of Lumiere to a sponge square. I used Gold, Bronze and Super Sparkle. Sponge a repeat pattern of color on a piece of white cotton fabric.

2 MIST THE FABRIC

After the paint dries, spray a mist of water on the fabric. This will make the next layer of paint flow more freely.

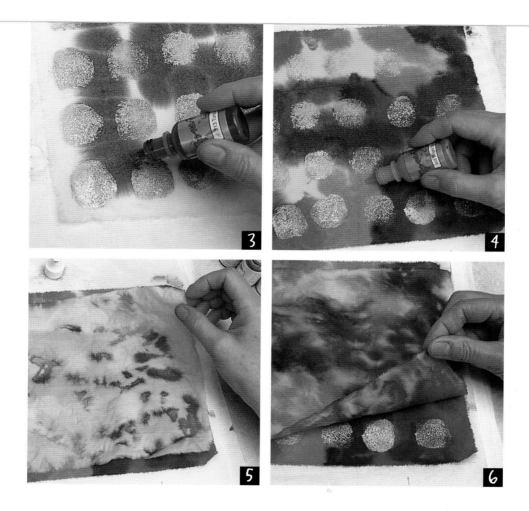

3 SQUEEZE TURQUOISE ONTO THE FABRIC

Squeeze Turquoise Dye-Na-Flow onto the wet fabric. Notice how the Dye-Na-Flow runs easily around the sponged Lumiere patterns. The thick metallic paint acts as a resist, pushing the Dye-Na-Flow toward the unpainted portions of the fabric.

4 ADD MORE COLORS

Apply additional colors of Dye-Na-Flow. The colors will bleed into a beautiful pattern.

5 ADD A SECOND DAMP CLOTH ON TOP OF THE FIRST

Place a damp piece of clean fabric over the painted fabric and pat it into place. Let both pieces of fabric dry together.

6 SEPARATE THE PIECES WHEN DRY

Pull the second piece of fabric off of the first one. Each piece of fabric will have a different finished look. Each can be used in creative projects or embellished further with paint and rubber stamping.

To take your design further with stamping, turn the page.

mixed media · recipes

a step further...

ROLLING ON A STAMPED PATTERN

Take this fabric a step further by using a Rollagraph to add bold patterned stripes, then dry sponge the edges to make it even more dramatic. Just follow steps 7–8 to add that extra touch.

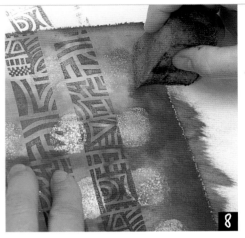

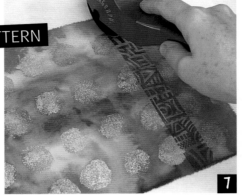

7

8

CLEANING TIP

Remove the Rollagraph stamp wheel from the holder and put it in a tub of water to soak. It can easily be cleaned with a manual or battery-operated toothbrush.

7 ROLL ON A STAMPED PATTERN

Roll the Rollagraph stamp wheel through Violet Neopaque that has been spread onto an uninked stamp pad. Make sure that the Rollagraph is completely covered in paint and roll it from the bottom edge of the design away from you to the top edge in a slow rocking motion.

8 DRY SPONGE THE EDGES IN VIOLET

Squeeze Violet Neopaque onto a sponge square. Blot and wipe off the excess paint onto a paper towel or a piece of "serendipity" fabric. Dry sponge the violet onto the edge of the design.

➡

The finished sample

The finished piece highlights the use of Rollagraphs and dry sponging.

recipe two:

Making Brilliant Patterns with Textile Colors

This project is a good example of creating a resist. A resist is any material used to block a portion of your work from accepting additional paint. By using a dense paint and letting it dry, you can squeeze a more fluid paint around it. I chose brilliant Textile Colors for the sponged stripes since they dry solid enough to create a resist for Dye-Na-Flow, a very fluid paint.

supplies:

- *sponge squares*
- *Textile Colors: Turquoise, Scarlet Red, Violet, Periwinkle and Russet (in plastic squeeze bottles)*
- *white cotton fabric with a high thread count*
- *fine mist spray bottle filled with water*
- *Dye-Na-Flow: Teal, Golden Yellow, Bright Orange, Magenta, Periwinkle and Turquoise*
- *roll of masking tape*
- *Rollagraph with patterned wheel stamp*
- *Sherrill's Sorbets: Mint and Grape*
- *Neopaque: Violet*

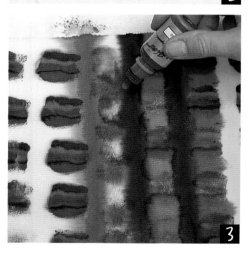

❶ SQUEEZE STRIPES OF TEXTILE COLORS ONTO A SPONGE

Apply a series of different-colored stripes of Textile Colors onto a sponge square. I used Turquoise, Scarlet Red, Violet, Periwinkle and Russet.

❷ SPONGE SPOTS ONTO THE FABRIC

Sponge the paint onto a piece of dry fabric. Repeat the sponging until the cloth is filled with striped patterns. Add more paint to your sponge if the color runs dry, or spritz the sponge with water to draw out the remaining paint. When you are finished adding patterns, spray the fabric so that it is wet.

❸ SQUEEZE DYE-NA-FLOW BETWEEN THE SPONGED SPOTS

Apply Dye-Na-Flow between the patterns with a squeeze bottle. I used Teal, Golden Yellow, Bright Orange, Magenta, Periwinkle and dots of Turquoise. Set the fabric aside to dry.

To take your design further with stamping, turn the page.

a step further...

ADDING ROLLAGRAPH PATTERNS

Take this fabric a step further by adding Rollagraph patterns between torn strips of masking tape. Just follow steps 4–7. If you are doing this technique on paper, be sure to use a low-tack tape to keep the paper from tearing.

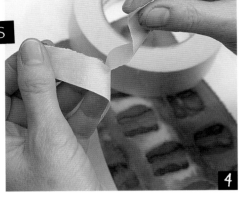
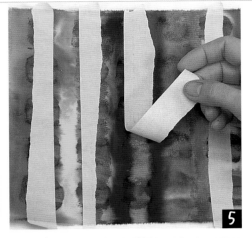

The Finished Sample

This sample is a vibrant mix of patterns and colors reminiscent of a tropical batik.

④ TEAR THE MASKING TAPE INTO STRIPS

Tear long strips of masking tape in half lengthwise. The uneven edges of the tape will add personality to the design.

⑤ TAPE OVER THE FABRIC

Place the masking tape over the brightest areas of the fabric and press the tape firmly into place.

⑥ ADD STAMPED PATTERNS

Roll the Rollagraph between the gaps in the tape. For the greatest contrast, use light-colored Sorbets in Mint and Grape over the dark areas and Violet Neopaque over the brightest areas.

⑦ REMOVE THE TAPE

Peel the tape from the surface to see the finished effect.

recipe three:

Adding Salt to a Wet Wash

Pigment-based fabric dye is the perfect paint for doing very wet or highly pigmented washes. If you add salt to this mixture, it pushes and pulls the paint in unexpected ways, leaving the surface quite textural. Experiment with different kinds of salt—rock salt, kosher salt, sea salt, iodized salt or pretzel salt.

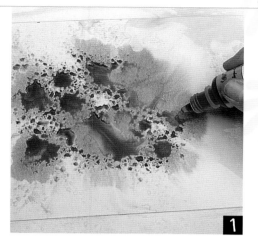

1

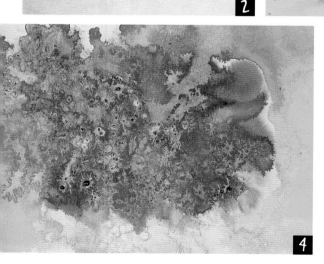

2

3

4

supplies:

- *piece of white Bristol board or watercolor paper*
- *fine mist spray bottle filled with water*
- *Dye-Na-Flow: Violet, Bright Orange and Golden Yellow*
- *salt crystals*
- *low-tack masking tape*
- *sponge squares*
- *Textile Colors: Fluorescent Violet, Periwinkle and Turquoise*
- *Lumiere: Gold*
- *uninked stamp pad*
- *Rollagraph with patterned wheel stamp*

① SQUEEZE VIOLET ONTO A WET SURFACE

Spray a piece of white Bristol board or watercolor paper on both sides with a water from a fine mist spray bottle. Squeeze Violet Dye-Na-Flow onto the wet surface.

② ADD MORE COLORS

Squeeze Bright Orange Dye-Na-Flow around the Violet. Squeeze Golden Yellow Dye-Na-Flow around the outer edges.

③ SPRINKLE ON SALT

Sprinkle Jacquard Silk Salt or any other salt onto the wet surface.

④ LET PAPER DRY AND REMOVE THE SALT

Let the paper dry completely and brush off the salt. Notice how the salt pulls up areas of paint and leaves an intricate pattern behind.

To take your design further with stamping, turn the page.

mixed media · recipes

a step further...

GLAZING COLOR OVER A TAPE RESIST

Enhance this colorful piece with brilliant glazes. Use low-tack tape to "resist" the paint in some areas and create stripes of transparent color in others. Just follow steps 5–10 to learn how.

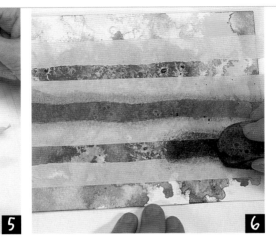

5 APPLY STRIPS OF LOW-TACK TAPE

Tear low-tack tape into lengths slightly longer than the piece of artwork. Apply the tape to the artwork in a striped pattern. Press the tape firmly into place.

6 GLAZE TEXTILE COLOR BETWEEN THE TAPED AREAS

Sponge Fluorescent Violet and Periwinkle Textile Colors between the taped areas. The Dye-Na-Flow plus salt patterns will show through the glaze.

7 GLAZE THE REMAINING STRIPES

Sponge additional stripes of Fluorescent Violet and Periwinkle on the remaining stripes.

8 REMOVE THE TAPE

Once the paint is dry enough, gently pull the tape from the design.

9 GLAZE TURQUOISE OVER THE UNTAPED AREAS

Sponge Turquoise over the areas that have been untaped. The Turquoise will unify the design.

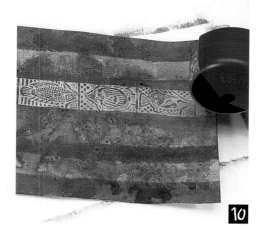

10

⑩ ROLL ON A PATTERN IN GOLD

Squeeze Gold Lumiere onto an uninked stamp pad. Roll the Rollagraph stamp wheel through the paint and then roll the design along one of the glazed stripes.

➡→

The Finished Sample

The glazes made with Textile Color unify this whole design while still showing the texture of the salt patterns underneath them. The single gold stripe makes a brilliant accent to the entire piece.

VARIATIONS ON FABRIC

•

This stunning variation on cloth uses many of the same techniques. The fabric was covered with Dye-Na-Flow and salt. Once dry, subtle glazes were applied between lines of tape. The borders were highlighted with Gold Lumiere applied with a metal applicator tip.

recipe four:

Creating Backgrounds with Textile Colors

Textile Colors make wonderful sponged backgrounds. They are highly pigmented, yet they are transparent. Sponging different shades of Textile Color directly onto paper or fabric gives you a brilliantly colored surface. When the edges of one color meet another, they blend and form subtle secondary colors.

1 SPREAD GOLDENROD WITH A SPONGE

Apply a line of Goldenrod Textile Color with a squeeze bottle onto white cotton fabric and spread the color with a sponge square.

2 ADD FLUORESCENT VIOLET

Squeeze a line of Fluorescent Violet Textile Color over the Goldenrod and blend the edges with a sponge.

3 SPONGE ON AREAS OF VIOLET AND SCARLET RED

Squeeze Violet Textile Color onto a sponge square and apply the color beside the Fluorescent Violet. Squeeze a line of Scarlet Red Textile Color onto the fabric and sponge the color across the surface.

4 GLAZE AREAS WITH SCARLET RED AND TURQUOISE

Sponge some of the Scarlet Red across the Goldenrod area. Squeeze a line of Turquoise Textile Color along the right edge of the fabric. Use a sponge to pull the color across the fabric until it is completely covered.

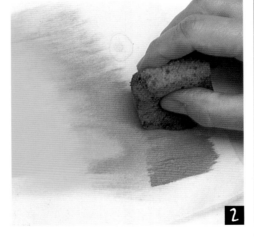

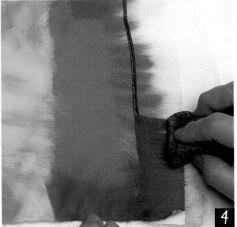

supplies:

- *white cotton fabric with a high thread count*

- *Textile Colors: Goldenrod, Fluorescent Violet, Violet, Scarlet Red and Turquoise (in plastic squeeze bottles)*

- *sponge squares*

- *Sherrill's Sorbets: Melon, Tangerine and Mint*

- *1" (25mm) flat brush*

- *rubber stamps*

mixed media· recipes

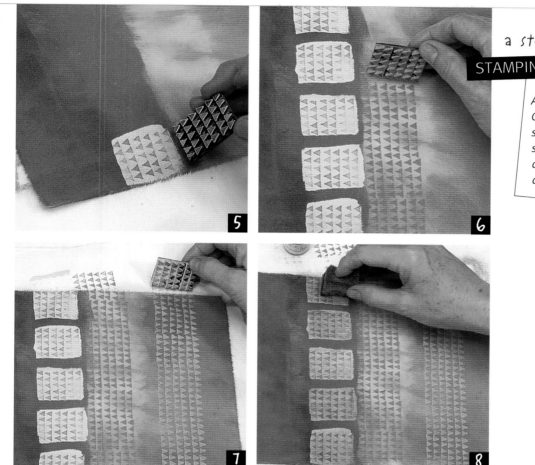

5

6

a step further...

A soft background of Textile Colors is great for layering with stamped repeat patterns. Follow steps 5–8 and notice how the contrasting colors can add extra depth to your piece.

7

8

The Finished Sample

By glazing over the bright Melon squares, the color is deepened. The squares blend into the finished piece more successfully.

⑤ STAMP INTO MELON

Paint a block of color with a 1" (25mm) brush and Melon Sorbet. Press a patterned stamp into the wet paint and lift the stamp, revealing the color underneath.

⑥ ADD MORE BLOCKS OF PATTERN

Brush additional paint onto the cloth and repeat the process until you have a row of textured blocks. Add another row below this using Tangerine Sorbet and the same rubber stamp.

⑦ STAMP MORE PATTERNS IN MINT

Stamp Mint Sorbet with the same rubber stamp. See how the cool mint color floats over the Fluorescent Violet below it.

⑧ GLAZE OVER THE MELON SQUARES

Glaze over the Melon squares with a sponge. Alternate using Scarlet Red and Fluorescent Violet Textile Colors.

recipe five:

Creating Backgrounds with a Battery-Operated Toothbrush

I got an idea to use battery-operated toothbrushes to clean my rubber stamps and my frequently messy hands. I also thought, "What if I used the toothbrush to move paint around the surface?" I ended up with little squiggly rows of paint. Experiment with a toothbrush and see what you can do.

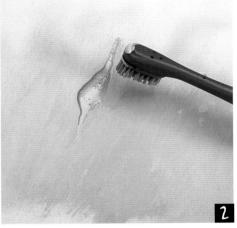

supplies:

- *Sherrill's Sorbets: Mango, Lemon, Grape and Blueberry*
- *battery-operated toothbrush*
- *piece of white cotton fabric with a high thread count*
- *Neopaque: White*
- *large angel stamp*
- *sponge squares*
- *Lumiere: Gold, in a plastic squeeze bottle with a 7mm metal applicator tip*

❶ SPREAD MANGO WITH A TOOTHBRUSH

Squeeze Mango Sorbet onto the fabric. Use a battery-operated toothbrush to move the paint around on the fabric.

❷ BLEND IN LEMON

Squeeze Lemon Sorbet over the Mango and move the paint with the toothbrush. Allow the colors to streak and blend into one another.

❸ ADD COOL COLORS AND BLEND WITH THE TOOTHBRUSH

Squeeze Grape and Blueberry Sorbets onto the lower half of the surface and use the toothbrush to spread the paint. Notice the strong diagonal lines being created.

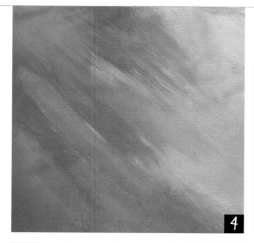

4

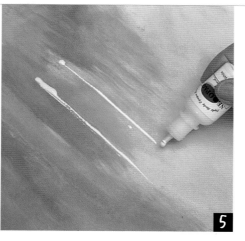

5

4 FINISH COVERING THE CLOTH WITH PAINT

Add more Blueberry, Lemon and Grape and blend until you have covered the entire surface with paint

5 ADD CONTRAST WITH WHITE

To add a little more contrast to the center of the design, squeeze two lines of White Neopaque over the other colors and blend with the toothbrush.

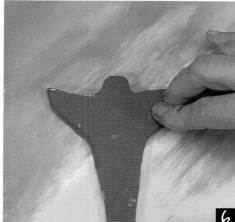

6

a step further...

STAMPING A CENTRAL IMAGE

This dreamy background doesn't need much to be transformed into an exceptional work of art. Often, a single image will do. Just follow steps 6–7 to add that dramatic finishing touch.

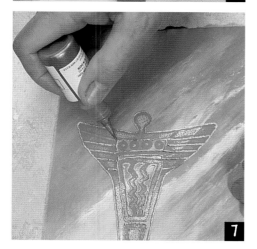

7

6 STAMP AN ANGEL ON THE BACKGROUND

Sponge Blueberry onto a large angel stamp. Position the stamp where it will make the best impression based on contrast and press it onto the fabric.

7 OUTLINE THE IMAGE IN GOLD

Highlight the outer edges of the image using Gold Lumiere from a bottle with a metal applicator tip attached. The gold highlights really make this image stand out against the soft background.

To make a matching frame for this piece, turn to the Angelical frame project on page 52.

mixed media · recipes

recipe six:

Sponging Color
Onto a Wet Surface

I use stamp pads as another painting tool. I don't usually use stamp pads the way they were intended. I use sponge squares on the stamp pads to apply color to a surface. For fun, try sponging from the stamp pad onto a wet surface. It is best to use highly pigmented paint when working on wet surfaces since the paint will lighten when it dries. I especially like permanent dye ink pads since the colors remain brilliant and waterproof after they dry.

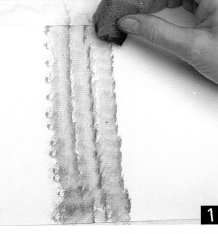

1 SPONGE INK ONTO WET PAPER

Spray a piece of white Bristol board on both sides with a fine mist spray bottle. Blot both sides with a paper towel. Rub a sponge square onto the surface of a Foxglove ink pad. Sponge the color onto the damp surface in an overlapping pattern.

2 SPONGE A SECOND PATTERN

Sponge Henna ink onto the Bristol board in a repeat pattern. This time I tried to make the pattern bolder.

3 ADD A WASH IN HENNA INK

Spray a fine mist of water onto the sponge containing the Henna. With the thinned ink, create a wash effect by pulling the sponge across the Bristol board.

4 ADD MORE PATTERNED WASHES

Sponge an additional wash of Henna on the other side of the Foxglove. Sponge Neptune ink onto the outer edges of the design. Spray the sponge and create washes with Neptune over the pattern and to the left side of the washed Henna.

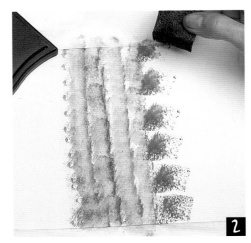

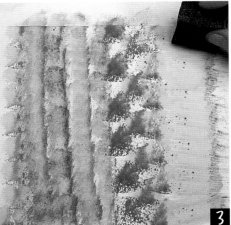

supplies:

- *heavy piece of white Bristol board*
- *fine mist spray bottle with water*
- *paper towels*
- *sponge squares*
- *Ancient Page stamp pads: Foxglove, Henna and Neptune*
- *Ancient Page dye re-inkers*
- *Neopaque: Violet*
- *toothbrush (battery-operated works best)*
- *sequin waste (available from florist supply stores)*
- *Lumiere: Sunset Gold*
- *piece of plastic window screen*
- *rubber stamp*

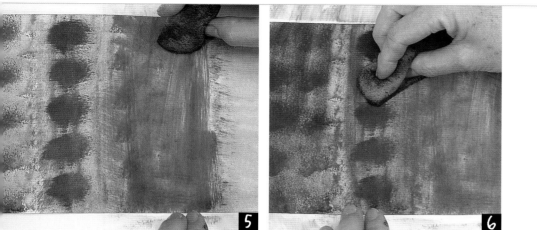

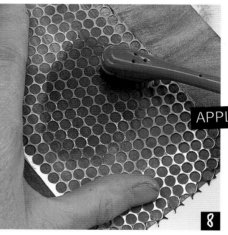

5 SIMPLIFY THE DESIGN WITH WASHES

This design is very busy. If you want to stamp over it, it helps to apply a series of strong washes to simplify the design. Squeeze a Henna dye re-inker onto a sponge and spray it with a fine mist spray bottle to thin the ink. Apply strong color over the washed and sponged Henna to create a dramatic background.

6 ADD A FINAL LAYER OF FOXGLOVE

Since this background is still very busy, squeeze a Foxglove re-inker onto the sponge. Apply Foxglove over the entire design to unify the final piece.

a step further...

APPLYING PAINT THROUGH STENCILS

Stencils offer a nice alternative to stamps when you want to embellish a background. Follow steps 7-10 to practice using two fun stenciling materials—sequin waste and window screen.

7 APPLY PAINT TO A TOOTHBRUSH

Squeeze Violet Neopaque onto a paper towel. Dip a battery-operated toothbrush in the paint. Turn the toothbrush on and brush most of the paint onto the paper towel. You want the paint remaining on the toothbrush to be quite dry, not wet.

8 BRUSH VIOLET OVER THE SEQUIN WASTE STENCIL

Place a piece of sequin waste (a hole-filled sheet of plastic left over from making sequins) over the orange area of the design. The Violet will contrast nicely with this color. Apply color through the sequin waste openings with the toothbrush.

9 BRUSH PAINT THROUGH A SCREEN

Squeeze Sunset Gold Lumiere onto a paper towel. Dip the toothbrush into the paint and again remove most of the paint onto the paper towel. Place a piece of window screen on the design. Apply the paint with the toothbrush through the window screen opening.

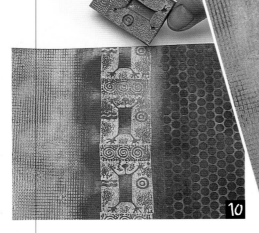

⑩ STAMP A PATTERN IN GOLD

Squeeze Sunset Gold onto a sponge and pat it onto a rubber stamp. As an accent, stamp a repeat pattern on the design.

↑ The Finished Sample

This piece went through many stages to get to this final design. Don't be afraid to keep playing with a surface until it works for you. This design went from busy to simple to finely patterned. Every layer contributes to the overall effect.

recipe seven:

Creating Scraped Patterns on Fabric

Scraping paint is fun, easy and exciting. I love to do scraped pieces. Look for different tools that can be used to scrape paint such as spatulas, notched tools, old credit cards or any other stiff tool that will move paint. Try different combinations of paints for a more exciting finished piece.

supplies:

- *piece of white cotton fabric with a high thread count*
- *Neopaque: Turquoise and Violet*
- *Lumiere: Gold, Halo Blue Gold and Copper*
- *Textile Colors: Fluorescent Violet and Scarlet Red*
- *wooden craft stick*
- *paint scraper or old credit card*
- *molding paste*
- *patterned rubber stamp*
- *1-inch (25mm) flat brush*

① SCRAPE TURQUOISE WITH A PAINT SCRAPER

Squeeze a few lines of Turquoise Neopaque 3" (7.6cm) below the top edge of the fabric and scrape them down with a paint scraper.

② SCRAPE VIOLET AND GOLD

Squeeze Violet Neopaque and Gold Lumiere onto the fabric in between the Turquoise stripes and scrape them down.

❸ SCRAPE COLOR OVER THE REST OF THE FABRIC

Dip a wooden craft stick into a jar of Fluorescent Violet Textile Color and apply the paint to the lower part of the fabric. Scrape it down. Keep adding and scraping paint until you reach the bottom of the fabric. Squeeze Scarlet Red Textile Color onto the last edge of the fabric and scrape it down.

❹ SCRAPE ON ACCENTS IN TURQUOISE

Squeeze Textile Colors on the upper edge of the fabric and scrape them toward the top. I started with Violet, then White but eventually settled on Turquoise Neopaque. Use the scraper edge to add lines of Turquoise to the lower half of the design.

a step further...

USING MOLDING PASTE FOR TEXTURE

Stamping into molding paste can add an interesting new texture to your painted surface. Follow steps 5–10 to create an elegant molding-paste border to accent this entire piece.

❺ BRUSH ON MOLDING PASTE

Brush a square of thick molding paste onto the painted fabric where the colors border each other.

❻ STAMP INTO THE PASTE

Press a rubber stamp into the wet paste and remove.

❼ FINISH STAMPING AND LET DRY

Repeat the process across the surface. Set the fabric aside for up to an hour until it is dry.

mixed media · recipes

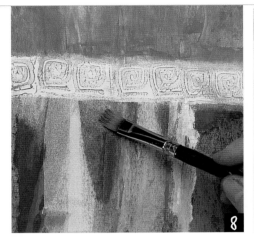

The Finished Sample

This is a bold, busy and colorful piece.
The textured gold band of molding
paste beautifully gathers together all
of the scraped colors below it.

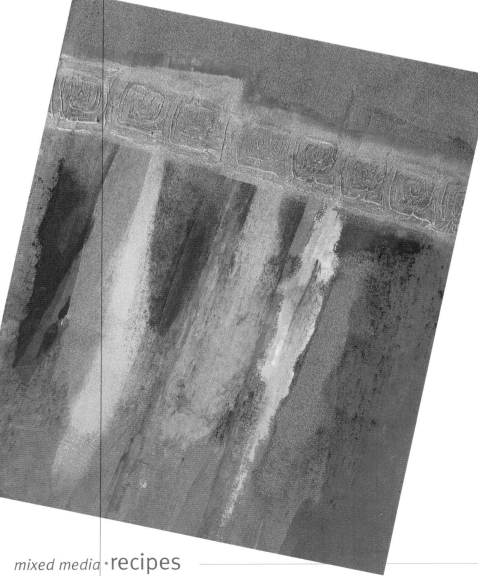

8 BRUSH OVER THE MOLDING PASTE IN GOLD

Use a brush to paint the molding paste design
with Gold Lumiere. Soften the hard edge of
the molding paste design by drybrushing the
Gold below the edge as well.

9 SPONGE THE TOP IN HALO BLUE GOLD

Squeeze Halo Blue Gold Lumiere onto a
sponge and apply the color to the top edge
of the surface. Leave a narrow strip of blue
showing along the border for contrast.

10 FINISH WITH COPPER HIGHLIGHTS

Drybrush Copper Lumiere over part of the
molding paste patterns.

Using Water-Soluble Crayons to Create a Background

There are a number of water-soluble crayons and pencils available. I have great fun using them in my artwork since they are clean and easy to use. Since I fly often, I draw on the plane with water-soluble pencils, then go over my drawings with a water-filled brush to blend the colors for a painterly effect. I also sponge color from the tips of the crayons or pencils onto my rubber stamps and stamp the designs on my projects.

supplies:

- *sponge squares*
- *fine mist spray bottle with water*
- *water-soluble crayons: Violet, Sienna and Black*
- *heavy cardstock or Bristol board*
- *tinted embossing ink pad*
- *rubber stamps*
- *Ranger Embossing Powder: Copper Pearl*
- *two to three sheets of plain copier paper*
- *heat gun*
- *Lumiere: Bronze and Copper*
- *Textile Colors: Periwinkle and Violet*
- *applicator squeeze bottle and 7mm metal applicator tip*
- *plastic serrated knife*

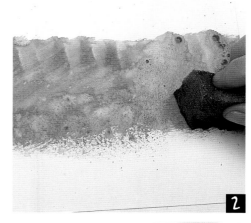

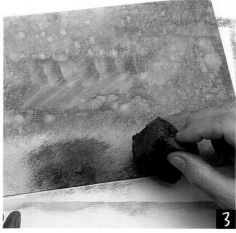

① ADD COLOR TO A DAMP SPONGE WITH CRAYONS

Spray a sponge square with a fine mist spray bottle. Rub the tip of a Violet water-soluble crayon on the sponge.

② SPONGE VIOLET ACROSS THE PAPER

Sponge a soft band of color across the middle of the cardstock or Bristol board.

③ ADD BANDS OF SIENNA AND BLACK

Sponge Sienna and Black above and below the Violet. You can adjust the intensity of the color by either adding more color or spraying the sponge with more water.

To take your design further with stamping, turn the page.

a step further...

USING METALLIC EMBOSSING AND HIGHLIGHTING

Deep, muted background colors look beautiful with bright metallic highlights in Copper and Bronze. Follow steps 4-11 to discover a few different ways to add the right decorative touch.

④ INK A STAMP WITH EMBOSSING INK

Pat embossing ink onto a large patterned rubber stamp.

⑤ STAMP THE IMAGE AND ADD EMBOSSING POWDER

Stamp the embossing ink onto the background. Pour Copper Pearl embossing powder over the stamped design.

⑥ REMOVE THE EXCESS POWDER

Tip the cardstock up and pour the excess powder back into the jar. Tap the edges to make sure there is no excess powder on the image. Remove unwanted powder with a dry flat brush.

⑦ HEAT THE IMAGE WITH A HEAT GUN

Melt the powder with a heat gun until the entire image is glossy.

⑧ STAMP MORE IMAGES IN BRONZE

Sponge Bronze Lumiere onto the same stamp used for embossing. Stamp the design onto the surface next to the embossed design. Repeat the stamping on both sides and let the image run off the edges of the paper.

9 GLAZE AREAS WITH PERIWINKLE

Squeeze Periwinkle Textile Color onto a sponge. Apply the color as a glaze over the stamped and embossed areas. You are intensifying the color. Add additional glaze with Violet Textile Color.

10 ACCENT WITH COPPER LINES

Highlight the central embossed image by framing it with applicator-tipped lines in Copper Lumiere.

11 FEATHER THE LINES WITH A KNIFE

Scrape the applicator lines with a plastic serrated knife to texture them.

➤→

The Finished Sample

This finished piece highlights a great combination of embossing techniques, glazing and applicator-tipped embellishments.

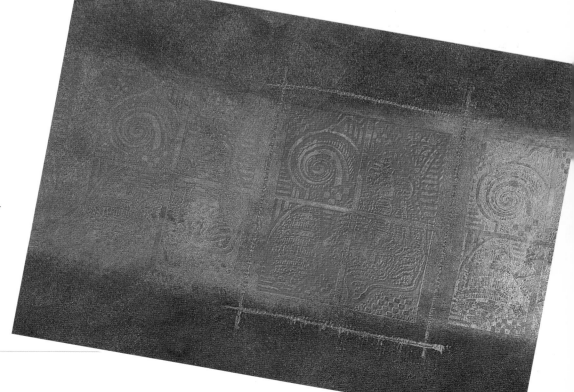

dding pizzazz to your work is easier than you think. Here are some of my favorite techniques. As you practice each technique, please remember that it is only on a piece of paper or cloth. Don't be afraid to take chances. Ask yourself "What if?" and then go and try it. Push the envelope. If you don't like what you've created, learn from the process and apply that knowledge to the next project you start. Soon you will be rewarded with work that has pizzazz.

Tip One: Create a Focal Point

The best way to make a plain background more exciting is to add a focal point. A focal point is the place where your eyes are mysteriously drawn again and again.

Like many of my pieces, this one uses a series of intersecting horizontal and vertical lines and a brilliant orange center to create an interesting focal point. Metallic highlights and strong patterns also create great focal points.

Tip Two: Increase the Contrast

A strong contrast between light and dark values always adds interest to your work. Most of this sample uses cool, deep colors. Brushing mint green highlights along the edges of the central shapes adds visual excitement and creates a perfect focal point in this piece.

3

Tip Three: Add Texture With Stamps

Patterned stamps are great for adding pizzazz to any work. When the contrast is low, as in this sample, stamping is an effective way to add depth and interest to a surface. Stamp light colors on dark and dark colors on light in the same piece.

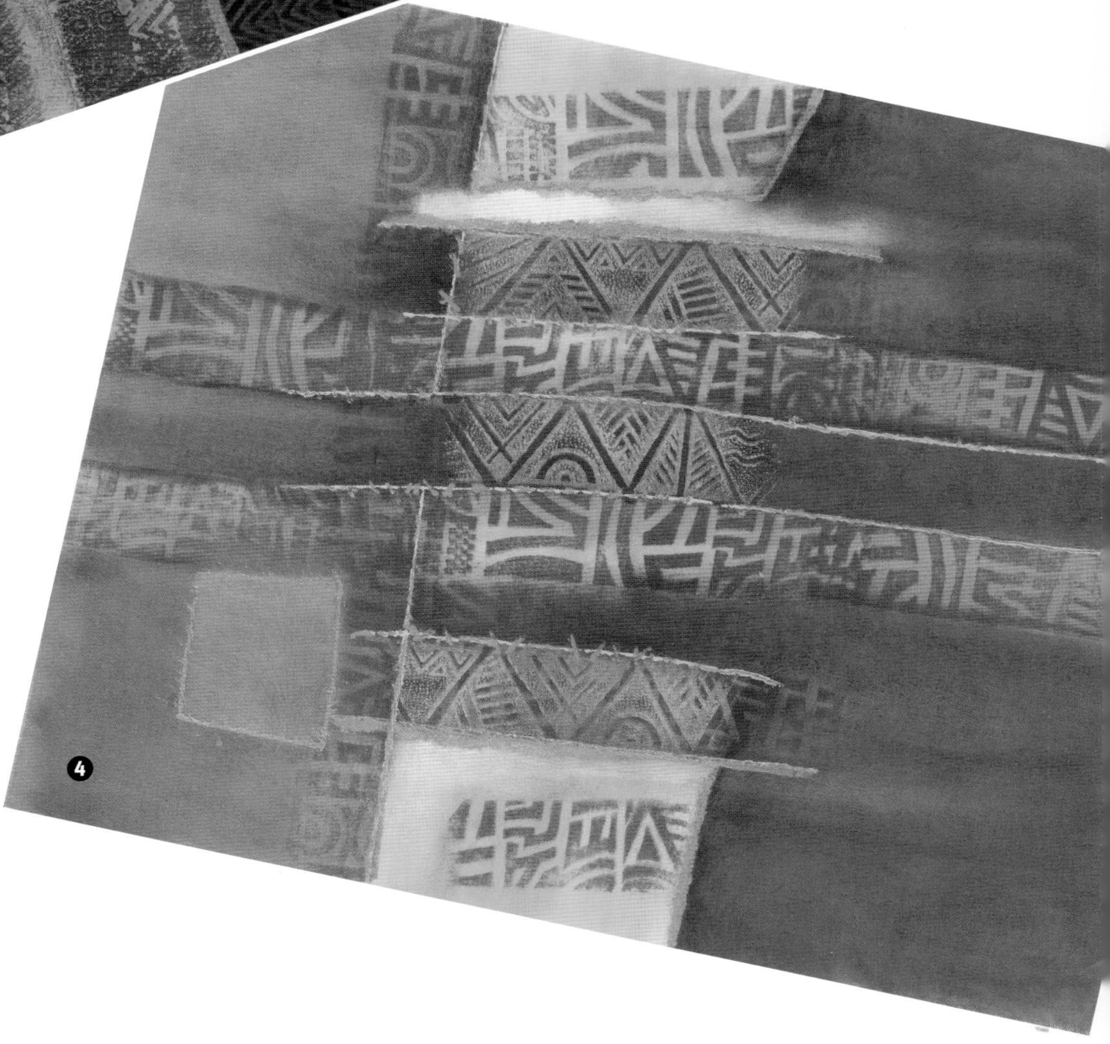

4

Tip Four: Use Complementary Colors

Complementary colors sit directly opposite each other on the color wheel; for example, orange and blue, violet and yellow, and red and green are all complementary colors. Because they are made of opposites, these color combinations are very dramatic. Try using various values and hues of these complementary colors in the same piece. This sample contrasts several shades of orange and yellow with their complements, blue and violet.

➡→

Tip Five: Accent Warm Colors With Cool and Cool Colors With Warm

If you are using mostly cool colors, add warm colors somewhere in your design. If you are using mostly warm colors, add cool colors. Adding a warm or cool accent color can generate a great amount of visual excitement to what was once an ordinary background.

←⊏

Tip Six: Add Accents With Metallic or Iridescent Paint

Nothing adds pizzazz like metallic paint! Just a little bit can make a project really stand out, especially against a dark background. Here, metallic highlights were added with an applicator tip and by drybrushing. You can also create more subtle effects by sponging over areas with iridescent Lumiere paints.

◂◂

Tip Seven: Tone Down Busy Backgrounds With Glazing

This sample started out with a uniform background of bright swirling colors. To create a focal point, I glazed over the outer edges with Periwinkle and Violet Textile Colors, leaving the warm center unglazed. Use this technique any time you want to simplify, focus and add pizzazz to your work all at once.

➤➤

Tip Eight: Block Out Shapes With Contrasting Color

You can fix any surface by sponging or brushing over selected areas of your design with Neopaque. Look for areas in need of added interest and paint blocks of contrasting color beside them. Here, blocks of deep violet make the nearby turquoise seem brighter.

Tip Nine: Use Repetition

Repeat colors, shapes, textures, lines or the same rubber stamp pattern. Doing this throughout a composition will tie it all together.

Tip Eleven: Mix Hard and Soft Edges

Hard edges create contrast and focus while soft edges pull your composition together. See how the figures in this piece play hide-and-seek? This element of mystery and surprise is created by painting over some of the figures but not others.

Tip Ten: Layer Your Work

Create a rich background by layering two or more techniques. Here I used dry sponging and stamping over a masking tape resist. Then I added more stamping, dry sponging and applicator-tip highlights. The overlapping shapes and colors give this piece great depth.

Tip Twelve: Highlight Selected Areas With Applicator-Tipped Paint

These three creatures stand out against the soft, dark background. I outlined each one with metallic paint squeezed from a bottle with a fine metal applicator tip. Applicator-tipped paint is wonderful for emphasizing borders and drawing attention to the most exciting part of your piece.

Tip Thirteen: Mix Different Materials

This wood and ceramic wall tile combines paint, stamping, paper and fabric collage, a Tyvek bead and textured gel medium. Experiment with your own interesting mix of materials. Unexpected combinations can spark whole new areas of creativity.

Tip Fourteen: Create Floating Shapes

Make stamped or sponged shapes "float" by surrounding them with a soft, free-flowing background in contrasting colors. This effect is especially dramatic when Dye-Na-Flow is allowed to run around shapes sponged in bright Lumiere. Adding a few dark Dye-Na-Flow colors enhances the effect.

TIP FIFTEEN: DON'T FORGET TO HAVE FUN!!

A journey of a thousand

miles begins with

one step.

•

Lau Tzo

mixed media
• stamping projects •

I hope you enjoyed the recipes presented in the first half of this book. Now you get the chance to put some of those techniques to work on a wonderful array of projects. You can try out all of your new stamping recipes on everything from wood to papier mâché to terra cotta. Elegant scarves, wooden boxes, a magic lantern, Southwestern-style pillow—there's something here to appeal to every creative desire.

The best part of the projects is seeing how the techniques you learned can transform any ordinary surface into an exciting work of art. I will also introduce you to a few great recipes for making different kinds of stamped beads from air-dry clay, shrink plastic and Tyvek. It is these sorts of embellishments that make a piece truly exceptional.

As you make each project, keep in mind the tips and suggestions I have given you. Turn to the pizzazz section on pages 44–49 for inspiration if a project needs some added spark. Constantly ask yourself, "What if?" Don't be afraid to try something new. Even mistakes are a chance to make great discoveries. Don't forget to have fun! That's what these projects are all about.

angelic
·frame·

it is very dramatic to "float" a piece of artwork in between two pieces of glass. Adding a frame is a simple and elegant way to display your art. You can choose any artwork for this project. I used the fabric that we created on page 34 to put in the frame. Tearing the fabric put the angel at an interesting angle. By stamping the frame with moldable foam tips, you can repeat patterns from the artwork you've chosen.

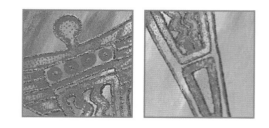

I saw the angel in the marble and carved until I set him free.

Michelangelo

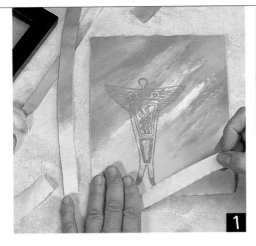

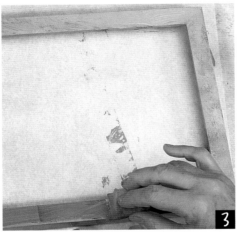

① TEAR THE FABRIC TO FIT THE FRAME

Tear a painted piece of fabric to conform to the opening of the frame. If you are using paper, cut the paper with a paper cutter or sharp craft knife, a steel-edged ruler and a cutting mat.

② BASECOAT THE FRAME

Brush Blueberry and Grape Sorbets onto the frame. Let the frame dry.

③ SPONGE THE FRAME WITH MINT

Lightly sponge Mint Sorbet over the entire frame, letting some of the original colors show through. Lightly sponge Melon Sorbet to selected areas of the frame.

④ HEAT THE MOLDABLE FOAM TIP

Heat a moldable foam tip with a heat gun. I chose a square tip that fit the size of the frame.

PAINTING TIP

I often shake up jars of paint and paint out of the lid with a brush rather than from the jar. I also sponge color from the lid when creating some of my painted pieces.

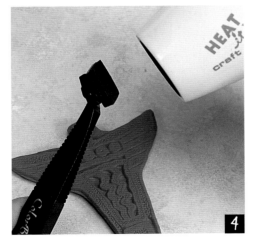

angelic ·frame

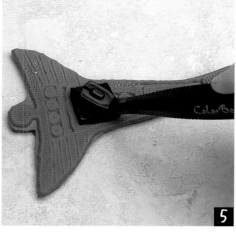

⑤ PRESS THE FOAM TIP ONTO A STAMP

Press the foam tip into the middle of the same stamp used for the artwork. Sponge paint onto the moldable foam tip and stamp onto a piece of scrap paper. If you do not like the image, clean the tip, dry it, reheat it and press it into the rubber stamp. Repeat the process until you are satisfied with the stamped image.

⑥ STAMP THE FRAME

Press the moldable foam tip onto the frame using a mix of Sorbets. Stamp warm colors over cool ones and cool colors over warm ones. This creates a floating effect.

⑦ ASSEMBLE THE FRAME

Clean the first piece of glass and lay the artwork face down on the glass. Place the second piece of glass over the first piece. Check to see that the artwork is centered to your liking. Secure the glass to the frame.

The Finished Frame

This frame took very little time to decorate, yet it adds magic to the piece of art inside.

tropical mango
flowerpot

transform a plain terra-cotta flowerpot into something incredibly eye-catching with paint, rubber stamping, a little raffia and air-dry clay medallions. Similarly decorated pots can be costly in boutiques and craft stores. Throw a springtime craft party and invite some of your friends over to decorate pots together. The techniques are so simple and dazzling that everyone will have fun. Use your finished pots to hold everything from fruit to flowers.

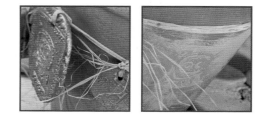

The world of reality has its limits; the world of imagination is boundless.

Jean-Jaques Rousseau

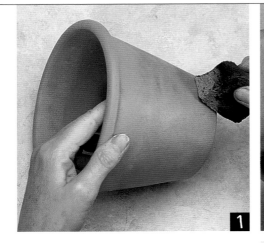

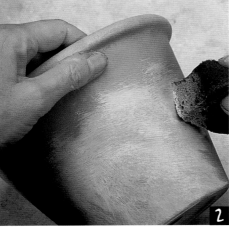

① BASECOAT THE POT

Sponge Tangerine Sorbet onto a flowerpot. Cover the entire pot, including about 2" (5cm) on the inside of the pot.

② DRY SPONGE THE SIDES IN MELON

Lightly dry sponge Melon Sorbet over the bottom half of the pot. The edges should have a softly feathered look.

③ SPONGE THE SIDES AND RIM WITH GRAPE

Sponge patterns in Grape Sorbet around the rim of the pot. With the same sponge, dry sponge a few random patches of Grape over the Melon on the sides of the pot.

④ STAMP A TROPICAL MOTIF

Sponge Mint Sorbet onto a rubber stamp and stamp a tropical motif in a few random places around the pot. Leave some space in between each stamped pattern.

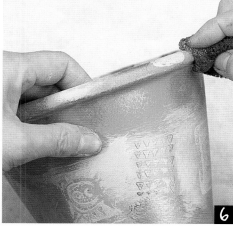

⑤ SPONGE MINT ON THE RIM

Sponge some Mint Sorbet over the Grape along the rim of the pot. This brings the color from the sides of the pot up to the rim.

⑥ ADD MORE PATTERN IN HALO PINK GOLD

Add additional rubber-stamped patterns to the pot at whimsical angles with Halo Pink Gold Lumiere. Sponge the same color onto the body of the pot and the rim. The metallic highlights will add a warm, festive glimmer.

You can stop here or embellish the pot further by adding air-dry clay medallions by following the steps below.

⑦ FLATTEN THE CLAY

Take a medium amount of air-dry clay and flatten it into an oval or round medallion with a brayer.

⑧ STAMP THE FRONT AND BACK

Place one or more rubber stamps under the clay. Press another rubber stamp on top of the clay. If the stamp does not cover the medallion completely, press additional rubber stamps around the center image. For this project, you will want to make three medallions: one large and two small.

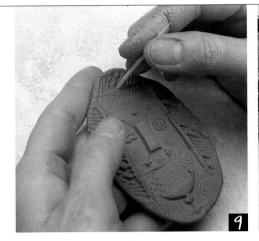

9 ADD A HOLE

Poke a hole through the top of each air-dry clay medallion with a toothpick. Rotate the toothpick in the hole to widen it. Set your medallions aside until they are dry.

10 PAINT THE MEDALLIONS

Brush Gold Lumiere onto both sides of the medallions with a flat brush. Add Copper Lumiere highlights with a dry brush. Let the paint dry completely.

11 TIE THE FIRST MEDALLION TO THE POT

Cut a long piece of raffia and tie it in a double knot high around the flowerpot. Leave at least 3" (7.6cm) of extra raffia on each end. Poke the end of the raffia through the largest medallion and tie it with a double knot. If the raffia bends when trying to poke it through the hole, wrap the end of the raffia with a small piece of masking tape.

Flip the pot upside down and glue the raffia to the pot in four or more places with a strong all-purpose craft glue. This will keep the raffia from sliding off the pot.

12 TIE ON TWO MORE MEDALLIONS

When the glue is dry, tie the smaller air-dry medallions to either side of the main medallion with more raffia.

13 DECORATE THE RAFFIA

Add the finishing touches to the pot by using a no. 2 detail brush. Paint spots of Blueberry Sorbet along the raffia tied to the pot. Fray the ends of the raffia with a ball-headed pin to finish the pot.

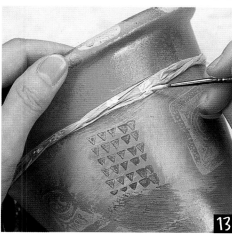

↓

The Finished Pot

You can fill your pot with more than just plants. In the winter, line one with colored cellophane and fill it with oranges, nuts and tangerines. Place one in your bathroom and fill it with hand towels and scented soaps.

southwestern
·pillow·

supplies:

- *piece of corrugated cardboard about 5" x 7" (12.7cm x 17.8cm)*
- *four to five flat, wide rubber bands*
- *Sherrill's Sorbets: Lemon, Mango, Tangerine, Blueberry, Grape and Mint*
- *sponge squares*
- *two pieces of black fabric torn into pieces about 7" x 10" (12.7cm x 25.4cm)*
- *scrap paper to cover your work space*
- *fabric glue*
- *paint scraper*
- *plain pillow in the color of your choice*
- *paper towels*
- *½-inch (12mm) flat brush*
- *7mm metal applicator tip*
- *Neopaque: Black*

playing with paint is an easy and effective way of decorating a pillow. This project gives you a chance to practice two fun techniques: using rubber band printing plates and creating patterns with sponge squares. I suggest you work on separate pieces of fabric for the main image in this project. This allows you to create a design you like before gluing it to the pillow. These pillows are especially attractive when grouped together in sets of two or three.

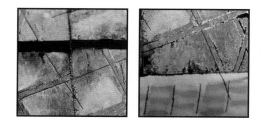

See things as you would have them be
instead of as they are.

Robert Collier

❶ MAKE A RUBBER BAND PRINT PLATE

To make a rubber band print plate, stretch flat rubber bands in a simple pattern around a piece of corrugated cardboard.

❷ ADD PAINT AND PRESS THE PLATE ONTO THE FABRIC

Squeeze Lemon, Mango and Tangerine Sorbets onto the print plate. (See step five to see how much paint to apply.) Pat the paint over the surface of the print plate with a sponge square. Turn the painted print plate face down onto one half of one of the pieces of black fabric.

❸ WORK THE PAINT INTO THE FABRIC

Flip the fabric so that it is face up and the cardboard is on the bottom. Press your fingers over the print plate to transfer the paint completely onto the fabric.

❹ LIFT THE FABRIC OFF THE PLATE

Pull the fabric off of the print plate. Notice how the rubber bands make an interesting pattern on the fabric.

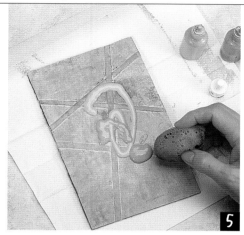

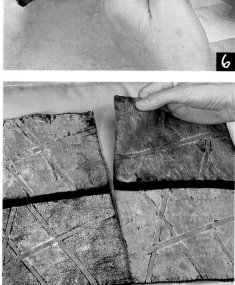

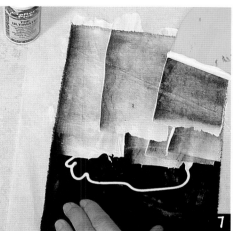

⑤ ADD COOL COLORS TO THE PLATE

Apply Mint, Blueberry and Grape Sorbets to the print plate. Pat the colors over the entire plate to blend them together.

⑥ MAKE A SECOND PRINT

Repeat the printing process on other half of the black fabric. Remember to flip the fabric over and work the paint into the fabric before removing the print plate. One half of the fabric will be printed in warm colors and one half in cool. Print a second piece of fabric in the same manner and set them both aside to dry.

⑦ APPLY GLUE TO THE FABRIC

Lay one of the painted pieces of fabric face down on a large piece of scrap paper. Squeeze a line of fabric glue onto the fabric and use a paint scraper to spread the glue over the entire back of the piece.

⑧ LAY THE FABRIC ON THE PILLOW

Glue the two pieces of fabric to the pillow side by side. You might find it helpful to have someone assist you when positioning the glued fabric on the pillow.

⑨ PRESS THE FABRIC INTO PLACE

Cover the fabric with a large paper towel and press the fabric firmly to the pillow. Let the glue dry.

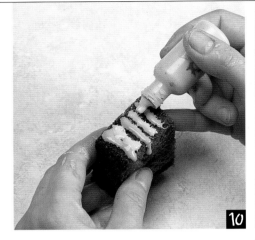

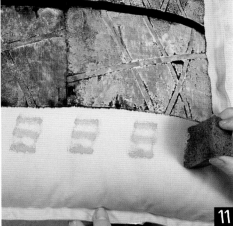

⑩ ADD STRIPES OF PAINT TO A SPONGE

Squeeze alternating stripes of Mint and Blueberry Sorbets onto a sponge.

⑪ SPONGE A BORDER ON THE PILLOW

Apply the sponge square patterns to both the top and bottom of the pillow alongside the glued fabric prints. Add more paint to the sponge as needed to get a good impression. Leave a space between each sponged pattern.

⑫ SPONGE ON A SECOND SET OF COLORS

Squeeze Mango and Grape onto the sponge square. Apply this new color scheme to the pillow between the first set of sponged patterns.

⑬ BRUSH ON WARM AND COOL ACCENT COLORS

Use a brush and Sorbet colors to highlight selected areas of the prints with blocks of warm and cool colors. By increasing the contrast between the colors, you are making the geometric pattern more dynamic.

southwestern · pillow

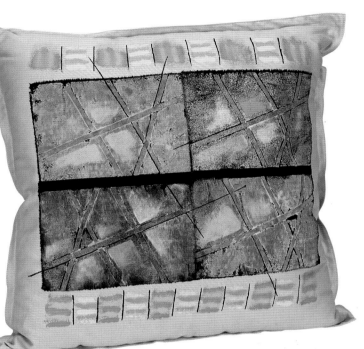

⑭ EMBELLISH WITH BLACK LINES

Place a 7mm metal applicator tip on a squeeze bottle of Black Neopaque. Extend fine black lines across selected areas of the pillow and between the sponge prints. This adds the final decorative touch to your pillow.

The Finished Pillow

You can adapt these same techniques to just about any fabric surface. Cotton canvas tote bags, wall hangings, place mats and table runners are all great items to decorate.

AN INTERESTING VARIATION

Here is another interesting way to use rubber band print plates. Make a rubber band print on white fabric using warm colored Sorbets. After the paint has dried, spray the cloth with water and squeeze Turquoise and Violet Dye-Na-Flow over the unpainted areas of the cloth.

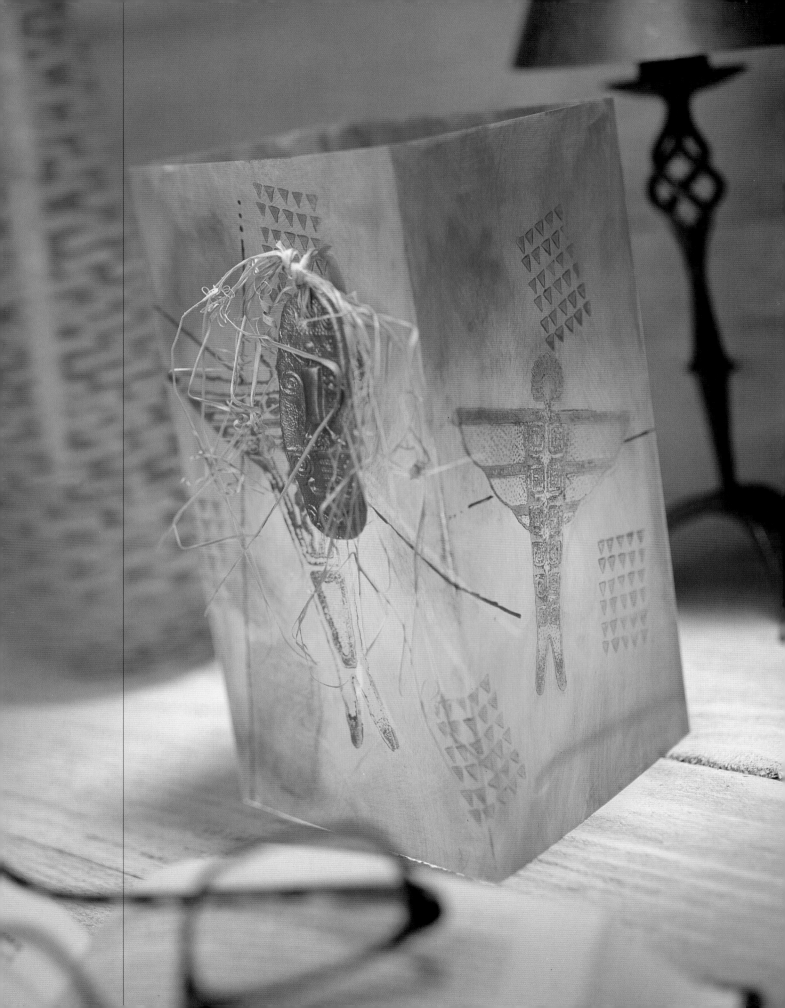

magic
·lantern·

t his wonderful lantern brings warmth and beauty to any setting. Made out of a stiff, noncurling vellum called Sheer Heaven, its translucency makes it an ideal material for lamp shades and lanterns. Light coming from behind the stamped images adds a whole new dimension to this project. The colors appear completely different when the lantern is turned on and off. Since the lantern starts out flat, it is easy to paint and decorate.

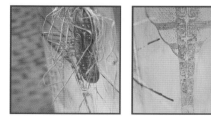

A journey of a thousand miles
begins with one step.

Lao Tzu

① SPONGE THE INSIDE OF THE LANTERN

Fold the vellum into four 4½" (11.4cm) panels with a 1" (2.5cm) flap at one end. Open the lantern flat on your work space. Sponge Fluorescent Violet, Violet, Periwinkle and Turquoise Textile Colors onto the inside of the lantern. Let the paint dry.

② ADD MORE COLOR TO THE OUTSIDE

Sponge warm Textile Colors over the first colors. I used Russet, Scarlet Red and Goldenrod.

③ STAMP ANGELS IN GOLD AND BRONZE

Stamp angel images or another motif of your choice on the outside of the lantern with Gold and Bronze Lumiere.

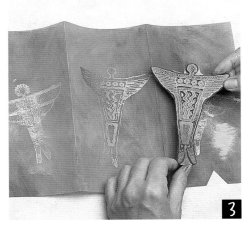
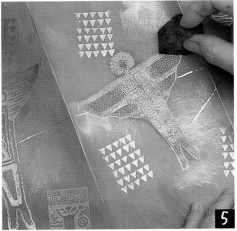
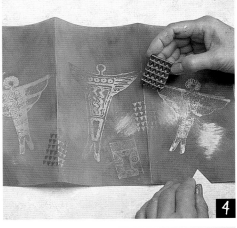
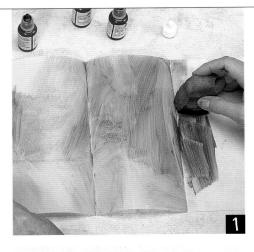
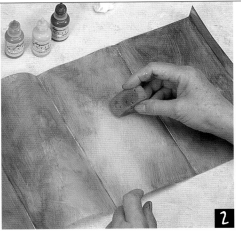

④ STAMP MORE IMAGES IN GRAPE

For added contrast, stamp over one of the angels with Grape Sorbet. Stamp smaller petroglyph patterns with Grape onto selected areas on the outside of the lantern. Add triangle-stamped patterns with Halo Pink Gold Lumiere in the remaining spaces.

⑤ ADD GOLD HIGHLIGHTS AND GLAZING

Attach a 7mm metal applicator tip to a bottle of Gold Lumiere. Add applicator-tipped lines across and on the diagonal of the lantern. Glaze over the Grape angel and one of the petroglyph-stamped images with Periwinkle Textile Color on a sponge square.

TIP

Place the lantern over the light base as you do each step to see how it looks when it is lit.

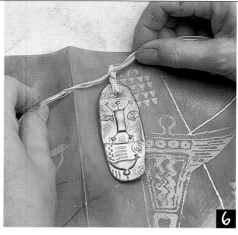

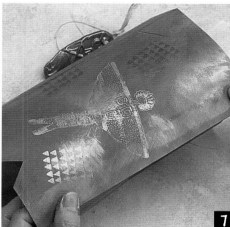

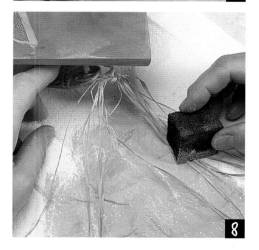

6 ATTACH A STAMPED MEDALLION WITH RAFFIA

Choose a spot for hanging a medallion onto the lantern. Mark the spot with a marking pen and poke two holes into the lantern with a needle tool. Thread the holes with a long piece of raffia and use a pair of double knots to tie on a medallion made of air-dry clay. (See pages 59–60, steps 7–10, for instructions on how to make a medallion.)

7 GLUE THE LANTERN TOGETHER

Apply a line of white craft glue to the folded flap of the lantern. Glue the lantern together by pressing the body of the lantern to the flap of the lantern. Put weight on the glued edge and set it aside to dry.

8 PAINT THE RAFFIA

Once the glued lantern is dry, place a paper towel under the raffia. Sponge Mint Sorbet over the raffia. Once the paint is dry, shred the loose ends of the raffia with a ball-headed pin.

The Finished Lantern

Light up your finished lantern with the small lamp or a battery-operated candle. This lantern is so easy to paint that it is the perfect project for children to try.

· tray ·
for all seasons

supplies:

- *Lumiere: Halo Blue Gold and Gold*
- *Dye-Na-Flow: Midnight Blue*
- *Neopaque: Violet, Turquoise and White*
- *small bowl to mix paint*
- *stir stick*
- *unpainted wooden tray*
- *sponge squares*
- *stiff foam plate or foam lid from a take-out container*
- *scissors*
- *ballpoint pen*
- *deep-etched rubber stamps*
- *7mm metal applicator tip*

t his beautiful tray can hold anything from art supplies to candles to shells from the beach. The tray can be adapted to match any color scheme and makes a wonderful gift for someone special. This project highlights easy ways to use handmade foam print plates to embellish decorative items. The relatively large size of the foam plate makes it an ideal choice for making patterns on large, flat surfaces such as this tray.

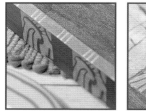

To begin, begin.

Peter Nivio Zarlenga

① MIX THE PAINT

Mix Halo Blue Gold Lumiere, Midnight Blue Dye-Na-Flow and Violet Neopaque in a small bowl. Stir the paint until you are satisfied with the color.

② BASECOAT THE TRAY

Make sure your tray is well sanded before you begin. Sponge the mixed paint onto the entire tray. This seals and colors the tray all in one step! Let the tray dry.

③ STAMP THE TRAY WITH A FOAM PRINT PLATE

Following the instructions on page 18, make a foam print plate. Sponge a mixture of Turquoise and White Neopaque onto the foam plate. Make a print on the tray with the foam print plate.

④ TOUCH UP BARE SPOTS WITH PAINT

If some of the image fails to print completely, use your fingers or a brush to add paint to the areas that need it.

⑤ STAMP ADDITIONAL PATTERNS

Make three large prints on the tray. Using the same colors, stamp a repeat pattern with a smaller rubber stamp between the three prints to create an overall design.

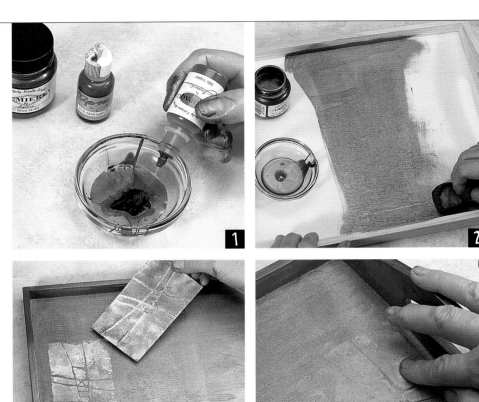

6 STAMP THE TRAY SIDES

Stamp on the sides of the tray in a random pattern. Apply the same color to the edges of the tray with a sponge square.

7 ADD METALLIC HIGHLIGHTS

Place a metal applicator tip onto a bottle of Gold Lumiere. Add applicator-tipped highlights to the edge and bottom of the tray.

8 SPONGE THE TRAY EDGES

Sponge Lumiere paint along the edges of the tray to add a bit of extra sparkle.

The Finished Tray

The finished tray is a gorgeous mix of luminous marine colors and gold accents. Choose colors and patterns that best complement your own home décor.

Protect the painted surface of your tray by coating it with a water-based varnish. This will keep your tray from being affected by moisture.

elegant
tower·box

supplies:

- *6½" x 6½" x 12" (16.5cm x 16.5cm x 30.5cm) papier mâché box*
- *Lumiere: Olive, Halo Pink Gold, Bronze and Gold*
- *Dye-Na-Flow: Midnight Blue*
- *small bowl*
- *stir stick*
- *sponge squares*
- *deep-etched rubber stamps*
- *Sherrill's Sorbets: Mint*
- *embossing stamp pad*
- *gold embossing powder*
- *heat gun*
- *molding paste*
- *½-inch (12mm) flat brush*
- *paper towels*
- *air-dry clay*
- *brayer*
- *rounded toothpick*
- *awl*
- *raffia*
- *ball-headed pin*

t his gorgeous box was easy to paint and a lot of fun to do. The challenge was coming up with a design that worked well with the height of the box. Stamping repeated bands around the box proved to be a simple and elegant solution. I then added texture with embossing powder, molding paste reliefs and air-dry clay elements. The box can hold a dried flower arrangement with the lid propped against the box for a nice decorative effect, or it can be filled with a bag of small treats or cookies to share with friends.

Imagination is the highest kite one can fly.

Lauren Bacall

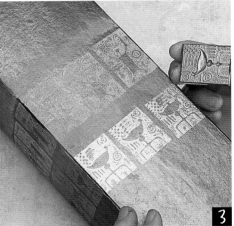

❶ BASECOAT THE OUTSIDE OF THE BOX

Squeeze Olive Lumiere and Midnight Blue Dye-Na-Flow in a bowl and stir them together. The Dye-Na-Flow thins the Lumiere enough to make a smooth, light basecoat for the box. Sponge the paint onto the lid and the entire box, including about 2" (5cm) into the interior of the box.

❷ STAMP A PATTERN IN MINT

Rubber stamp a pattern around the box using Mint Sorbet. With the leftover paint on the sponge, dry sponge color below the stamped impressions to soften their edges.

❸ ADD A SECOND BORDER WITH A DIFFERENT STAMP

With a different rubber stamp, do another row of rubber stamping using Halo Pink Gold Lumiere.

❹ EMBOSS AN ACCENT PATTERN IN GOLD

Apply embossing ink to a third rubber stamp with an embossing stamp pad. Stamp the image at a fun angle on the surface of the box. Sprinkle gold embossing powder onto the image and emboss the image using a heat gun. (For tips on embossing, see steps 4–7 on page 42.)

elegant tower·box

⑤ ADD MORE PATTERN IN MINT

Add a few more embossed accents around the box. Stamp the same image along the bottom of the box using Mint Sorbet and along the edges of the box lid using Bronze Lumiere.

⑥ STAMP INTO MOLDING PASTE ON THE LID

Apply a thin band of molding paste to the lid of the box with a flat brush. Apply a small amount at a time and press into the wet paste with a rubber stamp.

⑦ BRUSH THE TEXTURED AREAS IN GOLD

After the paste dries, paint the entire area with Gold Lumiere and a flat brush.

⑧ ADD BRONZE HIGHLIGHTS

Add some Bronze highlights to the Gold. Dip a flat brush into a jar of Bronze Lumiere. Brush most of the paint onto a paper towel (or serendipity fabric or cardstock) to create a dry brush. Hold the brush perpendicular to the surface and "whisk" the color onto selected areas of the painted molding paste.

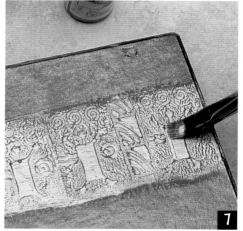

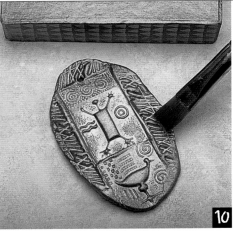

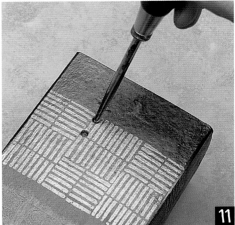

9 MAKE AN AIR-DRY CLAY MEDALLION

Flatten a ball of air-dry clay with a brayer into a flat oval medallion about 2" x 3" x ¼" (5cm x 7.6cm x .6cm). Place one or more deeply etched stamps under the medallion. Press additional stamps on top of the clay to texture it. Poke a hole in the top of the medallion with a toothpick. Set the medallion aside to dry.

10 ACCENT THE MEDALLION IN BRONZE AND GOLD

Once dry, paint the entire medallion with Bronze Lumiere. Drybrush highlights on the medallion with Gold Lumiere.

11 POKE HOLES IN THE BOX TO ATTACH THE MEDALLION

Select an area on the box where you would like to dangle the medallion. Take an awl and use pressure to make two holes in the box.

12 TIE ON THE MEDALLION WITH RAFFIA

Cut a long piece of raffia, slip the ends through the two holes and tie it to the box with a double knot. Slip the raffia through the hole in the medallion and make a double knot.

⑬ SPLIT APART THE RAFFIA ENDS

Give the raffia a loose, airy look by splitting the loose ends apart with a ball-headed pin.

➤

The Finished Box

Papier mâché boxes are great surfaces to experiment upon. Have fun creating your own unique combination of stamped patterns, textures and embellishments.

TEXTURAL VARIATIONS

•

This little black purse uses one of the same motifs with very different results. Here, a scrap of fun foam was heated and the stamp pressed into it for a dimensional look. Even on a busy background, this single image stands out.

elegant tower·box

freestanding
angel·card

t his is such a wonderful project because you can use it as a free-standing decoration on a mantle or shelf, or hang it as an ornament. Any doll-shaped or animal-shaped rubber stamp will work. Make the card uniquely yours by adding collage, buttons, beads, yarn, ribbon, cord or any other personal embellishment. This project includes a fun demonstration on how to make strong, lightweight beads out of Tyvek.

The best portion of a good man's life—his little nameless, unremembered acts of kindness and love.

William Wordsworth

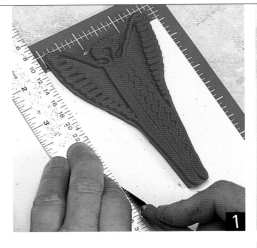

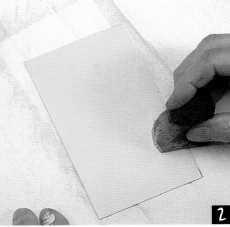

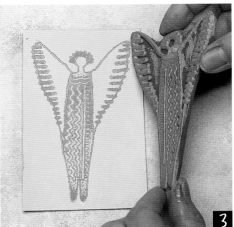

❶ CUT THE CARDSTOCK TO FIT THE IMAGE

Place a piece of cardstock on a cutting mat. Lay an angel stamp on the upper corner of the cardstock, leaving a ³⁄₈" (9mm) margin of cardstock beyond the edge of the stamp. Lay a ruler to the left of the rubber stamp and cut a rectangle around the angel with a craft knife. Cut a second piece of cardstock the same size as the first and glue them together with craft glue suitable for paper.

❷ SPONGE COLOR OVER THE CARDSTOCK

Sponge the back and the front of the reinforced cardstock with Melon Sorbet.

❸ STAMP THE ANGEL IMAGE

Sponge Blueberry Sorbet onto the angel stamp and stamp the image onto the center of the card.

❹ CUT OUT THE ANGEL

Trim around the wings of the stamped image, then cut straight down, leaving straight sides and a straight edge at the bottom.

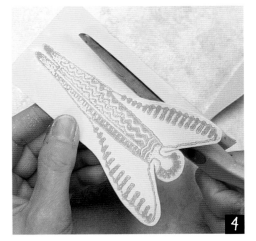

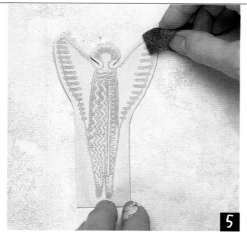

⑤ DRY SPONGE THE WINGS

Dry sponge Mint Sorbet around the edge of the stamped angel. Make sure that most of the paint has been sponged onto a paper towel or "serendipity" piece first and use a light hand when doing any dry sponging on your projects.

⑥ ADD VIOLET TO THE EDGES

Add Violet Neopaque to the same sponge and feather the color over the Mint Sorbet.

⑦ HIGHLIGHT THE BODY WITH GOLD ACCENTS

Paint metallic accents on the angel's face, body and feet with Sunset Gold Lumiere and a no. 2 detail brush.

⑧ DEEPEN THE COLOR ON THE WINGS

Deepen the colors along the edges of the angel by glazing the edges with Violet Textile Color and a sponge square.

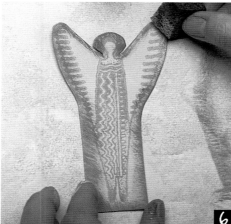

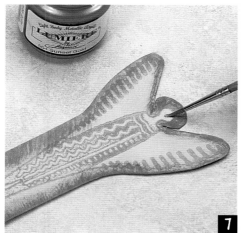

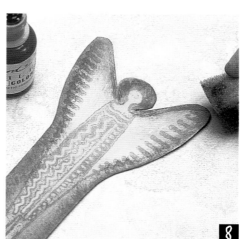

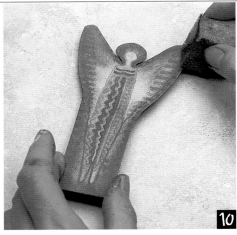

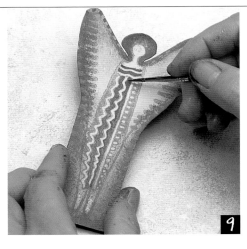

9 ADD MORE DETAIL TO THE BORDER

Add more detail to the angel's body with Violet Neopaque and a no. 2 detail brush. Paint a checkered border around the edge of the card with Violet Neopaque and add some more Gold Lumiere to the face of the angel. You are intensifying the color and increasing the contrast on the card.

10 ADD A VIOLET GLAZE

Deepen the color along the edges of the angel with another glaze of Violet Textile Color.

11 CUT A STAND OUT OF CARDSTOCK

Cut a long strip of cardstock slightly narrower than the card to make a stand for your card. Paint both sides with Violet Neopaque and stamp over the Violet in Gold Lumiere.

12 GLUE THE STAND TO THE ANGEL

Fold the cardstock in half and lay it on the back of the card. Use a pencil to mark how long to make the stand and trim the ends to the proper length. Glue the stand to the back of the card with white craft glue.

The basic doll card is complete. Create a matching beaded necklace to embellish your doll by following the remaining steps.

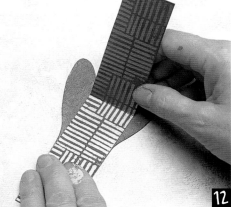

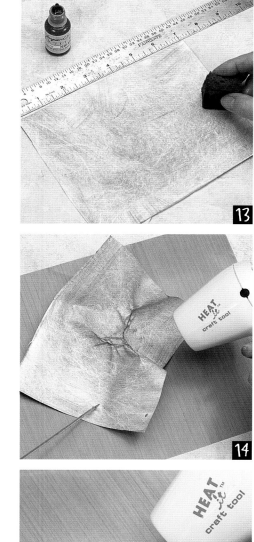

⑬ SPONGE COLOR ON THE TYVEK

Cut a piece of Tyvek about 5" x 7" (12.7cm x 17.8cm). With a sponge, glaze one side of the Tyvek with Violet Textile Color and the other side with Turquoise Textile Color.

⑭ HEAT THE TYVEK WITH A HEAT GUN

Lay the Tyvek onto an embossing craft sheet or other nonstick surface. Hold the Tyvek in place with a knitting needle (see the tip box below) or a wood-handled awl and heat it with a heat gun. Wear a mask if you are working indoors.

⑮ CONTINUE SHRINKING THE TYVEK

Keep heating and manipulating the Tyvek as you apply the heat. Notice how the colors intensify as the plastic shrinks.

SAFETY TIPS FOR HEATING TYVEK

Tyvek can be toxic if heated in a small space. Wear a mask or heat it outdoors. To safely hold Tyvek under a heat gun, I have created a special tool. Take a size 4 metal knitting needle and cover the end with sponge squares wrapped in duct tape. The taped end keeps the knitting needle from becoming too hot to hold. You can also use a wood-handled awl.

freestanding angel·card

16 PRESS A STAMP INTO THE TYVEK

While the Tyvek is still hot, quickly press a patterned stamp into it to texture the surface of the bead.

17 CUT BEADS FROM THE TYVEK

Cut the Tyvek into two pieces and round the edges with scissors. Notice how much the Tyvek has shrunk. Choose which piece will make the best bead for your angel card and punch a hole in the top with a $\frac{1}{16}$-inch (1.5mm) hole punch.

18 BRUSH THE BEAD WITH BRONZE HIGHLIGHTS

Dip a brush into Bronze Lumiere and brush most of the color onto a paper towel or "serendipity" piece. Lightly dry-brush the remaining paint over the textured surface of the Tyvek bead.

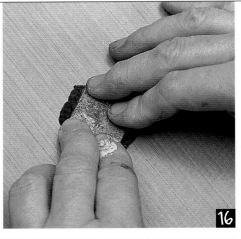

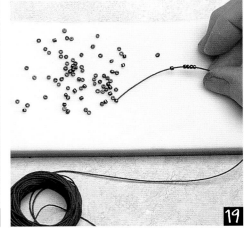

19 STRING THE SEED BEADS

String 1½" (3.8cm) of seed beads onto 6" (15.2cm) of stiff, waxed polyester thread to form a necklace. You may find it easier to pour the beads out onto a sheet of craft foam to keep the beads from rolling away as you thread them.

20 TIE THE NECKLACE TO THE DOLL

Loop the string of beads around the doll's neck and tie it close together to form a necklace. Use the loose ends of the thread to tie the Tyvek bead in front. Add more beads, fibers or charms to finish the necklace.

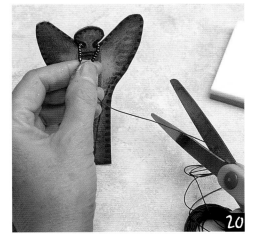

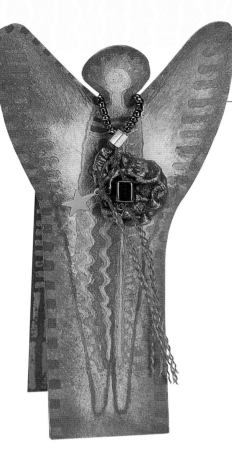

◄◄

The Finished Angel Card

Tuck the finished angel into an envelope and send it to a friend in need of some good cheer. Or prop it on top of your computer to serve as a creative muse.

FUN VARIATIONS

•

There are dozens of variations to explore when making these cards. Embellish them with shiny wire beads. Stamp the image on folded cardstock and write a short quote or message inside.

freestanding angel·card

gift·book
with necklace

- *piece of stiff black cardstock—at least 8o-lb. (17ogsm) weight*
- *steel-edged ruler*
- *narrow-blade craft knife*
- *cutting mat*
- *bone folder*
- *Lumiere: Halo Pink Gold, Sunset Gold and Gold*
- *Rollagraph stamp wheel*
- *Textile Colors: Scarlet Red and Violet*
- *sponge squares*
- *paper towels*
- *Neopaque: Black and Violet*
- *piece of deli or copier paper*
- *7mm metal applicator tip*
- *four sheets of cream text-weight paper*
- *stapler*
- *sheet of black shrink plastic*
- *scissors*
- *rubber stamps*
- *rubber band*
- *heat gun*
- *glue stick*
- *size 4 knitting needle with padded end (See the tip box on page 96.)*
- *20" (50.8cm) black rubber cord*

Very elegant stapled books are simple to make. Sponge, stamp and collage over cardstock to make a cover, then staple in some nested pages. They make wonderful pocket journals, sketchbooks and notepads. What makes this project special is the added surprise of a gorgeous beaded wrap that can be tied around the book or removed and worn as a necklace. The combination makes a wonderful gift for someone special.

If one has to work around what one has,
it makes it more unique.

Anonymous

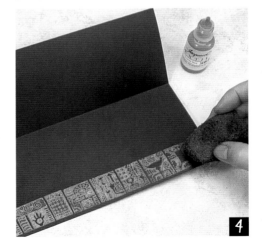

① CUT AND SCORE THE CARDSTOCK FOR THE COVER

Measure and cut a piece of black cardstock to 8½" x 6½" (21.6cm x 16.5cm) with a craft knife, a steel-edged ruler and a cutting mat. Measure and draw a pencil line 3" (7.6cm) in from the right edge of the cardstock. Lay a ruler on the line and score the line with a bone folder or embossing tool.

② FOLD THE COVER AND PRESS WITH A BONE FOLDER

Fold the left flap over the right and flatten the folded edge with a bone folder. The top cover will be ½" (1.3cm) narrower than the back cover of the book.

③ ROLL A PATTERN OVER THE BOTTOM FLAP

Apply Halo Pink Gold Lumiere to an uninked stamp pad. Roll a Rollagraph stamp wheel through the paint and roll the design along the right edge of the bottom inside cover of the book. Let the paint dry.

④ GLAZE THE PATTERN IN SCARLET RED

Glaze over the rolled design with Scarlet Red Textile Color and a sponge square.

gift·book *with* necklace

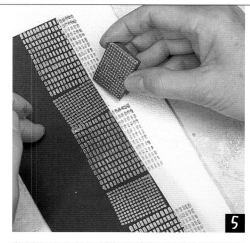

5 STAMP THE EDGE OF THE TOP COVER

Place a folded paper towel on the inside of the book to protect the design you have just created. Stamp alternating pattern stamps along the edge of the front cover using Sunset Gold Lumiere.

6 STAMP IMAGES ON THE FRONT AND BACK

Dry sponge Black Neopaque along the right edge of the cover. This will create better contrast with the bottom flap when the book is closed. Open up the book cover. Add some additional stamped designs to both the front and back covers with Halo Pink Gold.

7 EMBELLISH THE COVER WITH MORE DETAIL

Dry sponge Gold Lumiere around the cover. Attach a 7mm metal applicator tip to a bottle of Gold Lumiere and add applicator-tipped lines and dots to the front and back cover.

8 DECORATE A PAPER STRIP WITH SPONGED COLOR

Sponge diluted Violet Neopaque onto a torn piece of deli or copier paper. Add diluted Scarlet Red Textile Color or other colors to make an interesting piece of paper for collage.

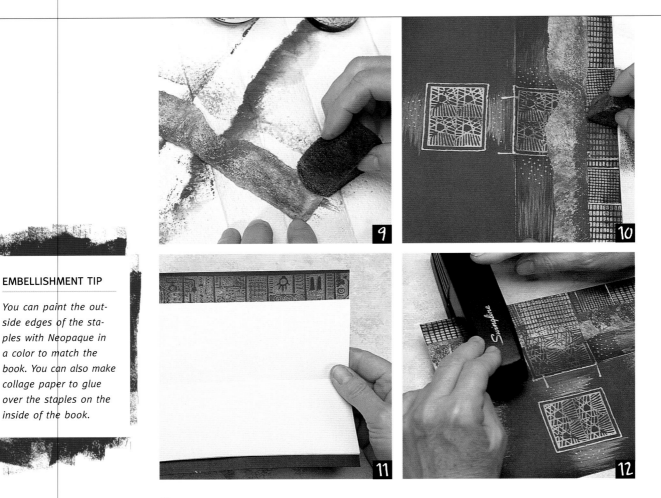

9 ADD GOLD HIGHLIGHTS

Sponge Halo Pink Gold highlights onto the collage piece.

10 GLUE ON THE COLLAGE STRIP

Glue the piece of collage to the book with a glue stick. Apply Scarlet Red and Violet Textile Color glazes to selected areas of rubber stamping.

11 TRIM THE PAGES

To make the pages for the book, cut four to eight sheets of paper to 8½" x 5" (21.6cm x 12.7cm). Fold the pages in half and press the folds with a bone folder. Nest the pages inside one another and insert them into the book.

12 STAPLE THE BOOK TOGETHER

Open the book up and align the pages properly inside the cover. You can use clips to secure the pages to the cover. Slide the pages with the cover facing up into a stapler. Staple the pages into the book along the fold.

Your book is finished. You can create a matching book tie with shrink plastic beads by following the steps that start on the next page. The book tie can also be worn as a necklace.

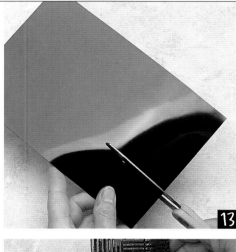

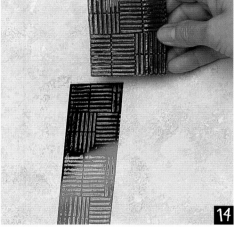

⑬ CUT THE SHRINK PLASTIC

Cut a strip of black shrink plastic to about 1½" x 6" (3.8cm x 15.2cm). You can also use other colors of shrink plastic. I prefer black or clear shrink plastic for making beads since these colors seem to adhere to themselves better than the others.

⑭ STAMP THE SHRINK PLASTIC

Sponge Halo Pink Gold Lumiere onto a rubber stamp and stamp a repeat pattern onto the shrink plastic strip. Having perfectly stamped images is not important. Let the paint dry.

⑮ ROLL THE STRIP INTO A TUBE

Roll the shrink plastic into a tight tube with the stamped pattern on the outside.

⑯ SECURE THE TUBE WITH A RUBBER BAND

Wrap a thick rubber band around one end of the tube to keep it from unrolling.

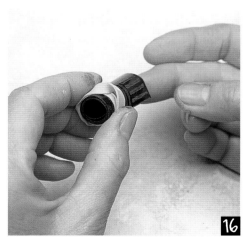

gift·book *with* necklace

HEATING TIPS FOR SHRINK PLASTIC

To safely hold shrink plastic under a heat gun, I have created a special tool. Take a size 4 metal knitting needle and cover the end with sponge squares wrapped in duct tape. The taped end keeps the knitting needle from becoming too hot to hold.

The knitting needle also helps maintain a hole through the length of the bead so that you can string it onto a cord after the bead is shrunk.

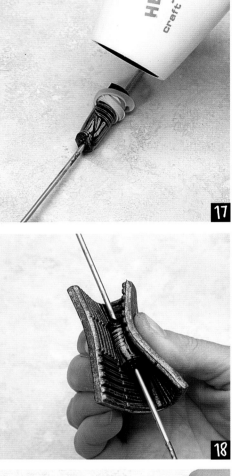

17 HEAT THE BEAD WITH A HEAT GUN

Insert the knitting needle through the hole in the bead and heat the shrink plastic with a wide-mouth heat gun. When the shrink plastic has adhered to itself through heating, stop and remove the rubber band.

18 PRESS THE BEAD INTO A RUBBER STAMP

Keep the tube on the knitting needle and heat it until the shrink plastic has shrunk completely. While the bead is still hot, take an unmounted rubber stamp and squeeze it around the heated bead. The stamp will create a raised textured on the bead. Remove the bead from the knitting needle to cool.

19 TIE THE BEADS TO A CORD

Create two more black shrink plastic beads. Make each one slightly different by changing the width of the bead or the stamped pattern. String the beads onto a black rubber cord. Tie a knot in between each bead. To make the knots snug, place a pin in the knot and pull the knot close to the bead. Tighten the cord with the pin inside the knot, then remove the pin.

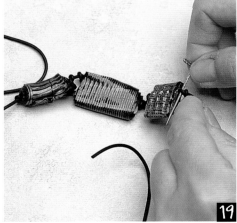

The Finished Necklace

Finish the ends of the necklace by tying knots on each end. If you wish, you can add smaller beads to the ends of the cord. You can substitute a gold silk cord for a more elegant-looking necklace. I used rubber because it is less likely to slip when used as a book tie.

The Book & Necklace Combined

Here is the finished booklet with the beaded necklace tied around it. The collage paper and necklace add wonderful texture to this project. Try doing this combination in bright colors or pastels for a very different look.

COLLAGE VARIATIONS

Collage works equally well with fabric as it does with paper. The feathered edges of torn fabric create a different look than torn paper. Collage is a great outlet for reusing leftover scraps of paper, ribbon and fabric. Collage can also change a composition completely. A softly sponged swatch can calm a busy design, while a scrap with a bold pattern can add spark to a plain background.

gift·book *with* necklace

aquatic
t·shirt

supplies:

- *foam lid from a take-out container*
- *scissors*
- *ballpoint pen*
- *sheet of deli paper or freezer paper*
- *dark-colored cotton T-shirt*
- *Sherrill's Sorbets: Grape, Blueberry, Mint, Melon and Lemon*
- *sponge squares*
- *rubber stamps*
- *no. 2 detail brush*
- *small flat brush*
- *Neopaque: Black*
- *7mm metal applicator tip*
- *Lumiere: Bronze and Copper*

t-shirts are the most popular clothing item in almost every country in the world. This project shows what you can do with a plain T-shirt to make it a special garment. I chose an aquatic theme, but you will only be limited by your imagination when you start painting your own T-shirt. This project highlights three great techniques: using foam plate printing, using a paint brush for adding details and highlighting your design with lines of applicator-tipped paint.

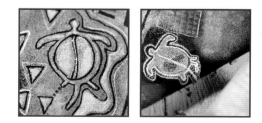

In the middle of difficulty lies opportunity.

Albert Einstein

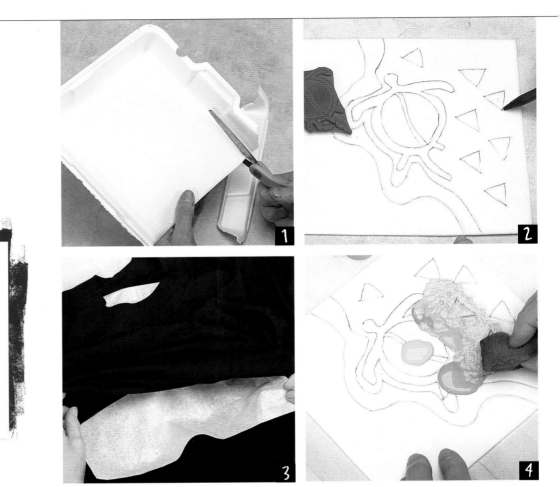

DESIGN TIP

If you want to preplan your design on paper, draw your design on paper and transfer it to the foam plate with carbon transfer paper. Go over the design on the foam with a ball-point pen.

1 CUT A SQUARE FROM A FOAM CONTAINER

Cut a large, flat square of foam from the lid of a take-out container or meat tray. I cut mine to 6¼" x 7" (15.9cm x 17.8cm).

2 DRAW YOUR DESIGN ON THE PLATE

Create a print plate by drawing a freeform turtle on the foam plate with a ballpoint pen. I adapted this image from a turtle petroglyph rubber stamp from "Impress Me."

3 PROTECT THE T-SHIRT WITH FREEZER PAPER

Place a large piece of deli paper or freezer paper inside the T-shirt. This prevents the paint from soaking through the T-shirt onto the back side.

4 SPONGE PASTEL PAINTS ONTO THE PLATE

Squeeze four colors of Sorbets onto the print plate. I used Grape, Blueberry, Mint and Melon. Sponge the colors across the piece of foam.

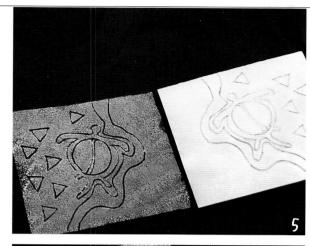

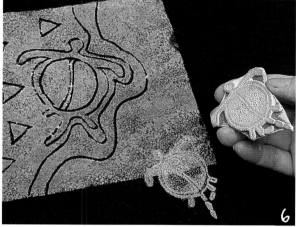

⑤ PRINT THE T-SHIRT

Place the print plate face down on the T-shirt. Press down firmly on the foam plate with your fingers. Pull the print plate from the T-shirt, revealing the print.

⑥ STAMP ON SMALLER IMAGES

Rubber stamp a matching turtle over the print with Lemon Sorbet. Stamp two more turtles around the edges of the print.

⑦ DRY SPONGE THE EDGES OF THE PRINT

To soften the edges of the main image, dry sponge several Sorbet colors around the print and stamped images.

⑧ ADD COLOR AND CONTRAST

To increase the color and contrast, use a no. 2 detail brush to highlight the large turtle's body in Mint and Grape. Paint over the long wavy line in Melon. Fill in the small triangles with several colors. Paint over the original outlines in the main design in Black Neopaque.

⑨ OUTLINE THE IMAGES WITH APPLICATOR-TIPPED LINES

Attach 7mm metal applicator tips to squeeze bottles of Melon, Mint and Grape Sorbets. Outline some triangles and the smaller turtles with applicator-tipped lines. Extend the center wavy lines beyond the print. Add Bronze Lumiere accent lines to the center wavy line.

⑩ ENHANCE THE DESIGN WITH MORE PATTERN

I looked at the T-shirt and knew that I needed to keep adding stronger color to make it work. I felt that the square shape of the main print wasn't exciting enough. To make the design more dramatic, sponge Bronze Lumiere onto a triangle pattern stamp. Stamp the pattern diagonally over selected areas of the T-shirt. Add dry-sponged areas of Bronze along the edges.

⑪ SPONGE ON MORE METALLIC HIGHLIGHTS

Paint blocks of Black Neopaque around some of the smaller turtles to break up the square pattern of the print. Pump up the color of the paint by sponging on more highlights in Bronze and Copper Lumiere.

⑫ ADD FINAL EMBELLISHMENTS

Add lines and bands of Black with a detail brush where you think the design needs more contrast. Add applicator-tipped dots of Bronze and Copper to the turtles. These final touches really add sparkle to the T-shirt. Once the shirt is dry, heat set the paints by ironing over the back of the design with a steam iron.

COVERING A PAINT SPOT ON A GARMENT

I try to be careful when creating my projects, but I often get paint spots on the garments that I wear. An easy way to cover a paint spot is to rubber stamp or sponge over the spot with an interesting pattern. This adds pizzazz to the garment and it often becomes one of my favorite pieces of clothing. Here's one clever way to cover a paint spot on a shirt.

❶ STAMP OVER THE SPOT

Slide a piece of stiff cardboard inside the shirt under the paint spot. Stamp over the spot with a design and fabric paint that coordinates with the color of the shirt.

❷ OUTLINE THE IMAGE

Apply an applicator-tipped line of Bronze Lumiere around the stamped image. The metallic paint makes a nice accent.

❸ ADD HIGHLIGHTS

Use a detail brush to highlight the center of the stamped image in a bright complementary color.

➤→

The Final Shirt

If you are not used to painting outside the lines, this project is a great one to practice upon. As you can see by the progression of steps, there are plenty of tricks you can use to make a plain design into something extraordinary. Don't be afraid to take some risks to make the finished project beautiful.

serendipity
wall·hanging

supplies:

- plain fabric place mat (a sturdy, tightly woven one works best)
- assorted scraps of painted "serendipity" fabric (See the tip box on page 14.)
- fabric scissors
- ballpoint pen
- fabric glue
- sponge squares
- rubber stamps
- Sherrill's Sorbets: Mint, Melon and Mango
- flat brush
- ½" (1.3cm) wooden dowel, cut 2" (5cm) wider than the short edge of the place mat
- braided or crocheted cord

f abric place mats are the perfect "no-sew" foundation for gorgeous wall hangings. Just glue a collage of colorful fabric scraps on top of the place mat for a quick, vibrant piece of art. You can buy place mats in a variety of colors and sizes at most home goods stores. Save all your spare scraps of stamped and painted fabric or use some of the samples created in the first half of this book. This wall hanging is fun to make and will put all of your "serendipity" fabric to good use.

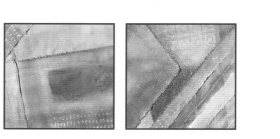

The flower that blooms in adversity is the most rare and beautiful flower of all.

Chinese proverb

① ARRANGE FABRIC PIECES ON THE PLACE MAT

Arrange several pieces of stamped and painted fabric on the place mat. Look for interesting color combinations and patterns as you play with arranging the different pieces.

② DEVELOP A COMPOSITION

Try different color combinations and angles. I like how this layout mixes warm and cool colors. The narrow strip of fabric set at an angle also adds some excitement.

③ REFINE YOUR DESIGN

Continue adding fabric that creates a unified mix of colors and patterns. Try repeating some elements. I chose to add two more diagonal strips to go with the first one.

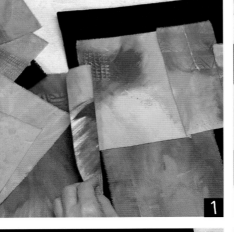

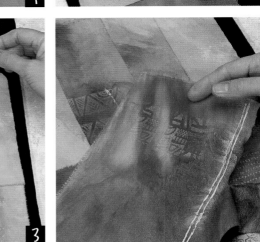

④ TEAR THE FABRIC TO FIT THE SPACE

Tear fabric pieces to fit in the final layout. As you go, even up the edges along the top of the place mat. You may find it helpful to mark with a pen where you need to tear a piece of fabric to make it fit. Leave a 3" to 4" (7.6cm to 10.2cm) margin undecorated at the top of the place mat. This will wrap around the dowel hanger.

⑤ GLUE THE FABRIC TO THE PLACE MAT

Turn each fabric piece face down and squeeze a line of fabric glue along the edges. It is not necessary to cover the entire piece of fabric with glue. Start gluing fabric pieces onto the place mat. Layer smaller fabric pieces on top of the larger ones.

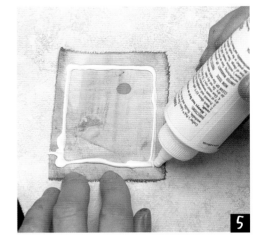

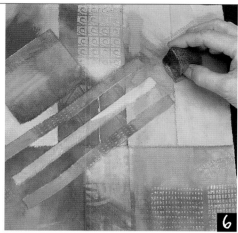

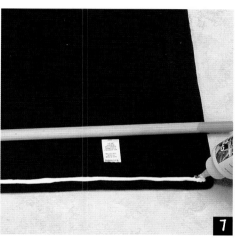

6 SPONGE AND STAMP ON MORE COLOR

After all of the pieces have been glued to the place mat, sponge additional paint on the design. Rubber stamp additional patterns in selected areas. Look for ways to increase the contrast. Adding cool Mint Sorbet helps make the warm Mango and Melon Sorbet stripes stand out.

7 GLUE THE PLACE MAT TO THE DOWEL

Paint 2" (5cm) of each end of the dowel in a color of your choice. Apply a thick line of fabric glue along the top of the place mat. Turn the glued edge of the place mat down over the dowel and onto the body of the place mat. Press the glue into place and weight it down firmly until it dries.

➤

The Finished Wall Hanging

Make a cord to hang your masterpiece. You can purchase cord in a store or make your own by crocheting, braiding or using a technique of your choice. This project offers endless creative possibilities. Even children can do this project with supervision since it is easy and requires no sewing.

treasure·box

supplies:

- 6½" x 6½" x 7" (16.5cm x 16.5cm x 17.8cm) unpainted wooden box
- Lumiere: Halo Pink Gold and Sunset Gold
- sponge squares
- extra-thick craft foam
- Sherrill's Sorbets: Melon, Mango and Tangerine
- Neopaque: Violet, Turquoise and White
- uninked stamp pad
- Rollagraph stamp
- Textile Color: Periwinkle
- 7mm metal applicator tip
- terra-cotta air-dry clay
- ½-inch (12mm) flat brush
- rubber stamps
- heavy-duty craft glue

this is a wonderful box to hold all of your special treasures. When looking at the step-by-step instructions, realize that you can stop at any point if you are satisfied with the results. I chose to decorate this box with glazing techniques, Rollagraph images, air-dry clay embellishments and applicator-tipped lines. You can also add collage, beads, yarn, cord, ribbon or any other embellishments you want. Choose your own special colors and techniques to make the box uniquely yours.

Live each day at a time and make it
your masterpiece.

Anonymous

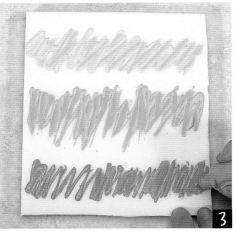

1 BASECOAT THE BOX

Basecoat a wooden box using Halo Pink Gold Lumiere. Use a sponge square to apply the paint. This seals and decorates the box all in one step! Let the box dry.

2 CUT THE FOAM TO SIZE

Cut a piece of extra-thick craft foam the same size as the side of the box.

3 ADD PAINT TO THE FOAM BLOCK

Apply Melon, Mango and Tangerine Sorbets from applicator bottles to the foam.

4 PRINT ON THE SIDE OF THE BOX

Place the foam sheet on the box and make a print by pressing down firmly.

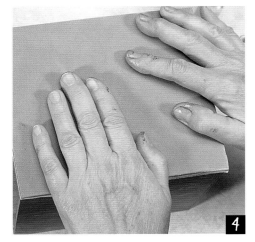

treasure·box

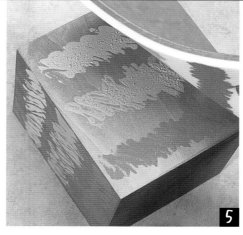

5 PRINT OVER THE REST OF THE BOX

Make prints on all of the sides and the lid of the box. You can see the print as I lift the foam. Let the prints dry.

6 ROLL A PATTERN OVER THE BOX

Apply Violet Neopaque to an uninked stamp pad. Roll a Rollagraph through the paint and then onto the box and lid.

7 ADD MORE BANDS OF PURPLE TO COVER THE BOX

Mix Turquoise and White Neopaque to the Violet on the stamp pad. Roll more Rollagraph stripes on the box. Let the paint dry.

8 UNIFY THE COLORS WITH A PERIWINKLE GLAZE

Sponge glaze the entire box with Periwinkle Textile Color to unify the Rollagraph stripes. Notice how the previous layers of color show through, adding depth and texture to the surface.

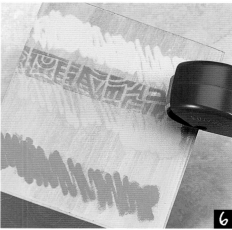

treasure · box

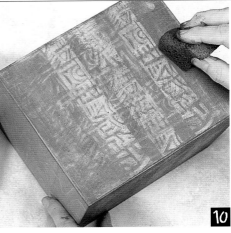

⑨ HIGHLIGHT THE BOX WITH METALLIC PAINTS

You could stop after the last step, but gold metallic highlights will add further interest to the box. Apply Rollagraph patterns to the box and lid with Sunset Gold Lumiere.

⑩ BLEND IN THE PATTERNS WITH A FINAL GLAZE

To make the Sunset Gold highlights more subtle, dry sponge Violet Neopaque onto the box.

⑪ ADD WARMTH WITH A TOUCH OF TANGERINE

To bring up the warm colors as an accent, apply a single band of Tangerine Sorbet with a Rollagraph along the top and sides of the box.

⑫ EMBELLISH THE LID

Apply a gold stripe with a Rollagraph along the sides and top of the box using Sunset Gold Lumiere. Attach a metal applicator tip to a bottle of Sunset Gold and add fine accent lines about ⅛" (3mm) from the gold stripe.

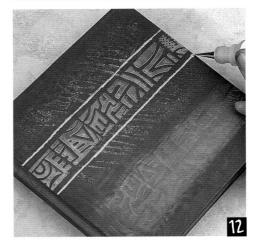

treasure · box

The Finished Box

The subtle layers of deep orange, purple and gold make this treasure box extra special. For added interest, glaze the inside of the box with matching Halo Pink Gold.

⓲ STAMP AIR-DRY CLAY MEDALLIONS

Create flat medallions using air-dry clay. Shape the medallion and press rubber stamps into the moist clay.

⓮ PAINT THE MEDALLIONS

Paint the medallions after they are dry with Halo Pink Gold Lumiere and a brush.

⓯ SPONGE ON VIOLET HIGHLIGHTS

Dry sponge Violet Neopaque on the edges of the medallions. Glue the finished medallions to the box lid with heavy-duty craft glue.

treasure · box

primavera
·scarf·

supplies:

- *30" x 30" (76.2cm x 76.2cm) China silk scarf*
- *piece of illustration board larger than the scarf or several sheets of deli paper*
- *fine mist spray bottle with water*
- *Dye-Na-Flow: Teal, Violet and Golden Yellow*
- *large grain salt crystals*
- *masking tape*
- *sponge squares*
- *Textile Colors: Periwinkle and Turquoise*
- *Lumiere: Bronze*
- *Rollagraph stamp*
- *uninked stamp pad*
- *Sherrill's Sorbet: Mint*
- *rubber stamps*
- *7mm metal applicator tip*

t his scarf is dramatic, beautiful and easy to do. Scarves are wonderful accessories. They can be tied around the neck, through belt loops
and onto purses to dress up any outfit. They can be wrapped around lamp
shades to add a special mood to a room or tied around packages to make
a colorful gift wrap. Trim your scarves with appliqué, beads, yarn, tassels,
cord or other embellishments to make them even more interesting.

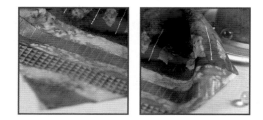

We know what we are, but know not
what we may be.

William Shakespeare

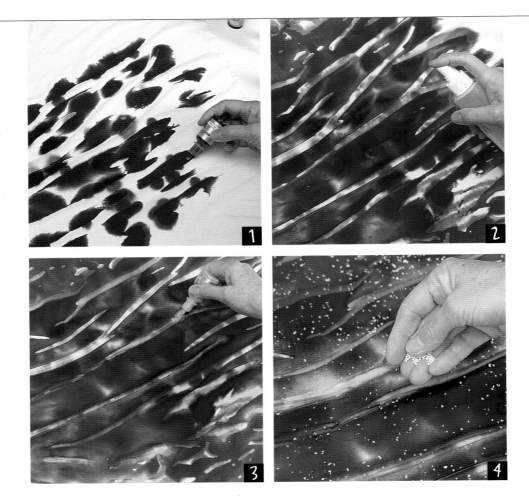

① SQUEEZE TEAL AND VIOLET ON A WET SCARF

Lay a 30" x 30" (76.2cm x 76.2cm) silk scarf on a large piece of illustration board or several pieces of deli paper—enough to cover your work surface. Spray the scarf with a fine mist spray bottle. Make sure the entire scarf is wet, not just damp. Squeeze broken rows of Teal and Violet Dye-Na-Flow on the scarf.

② ADD MORE COLOR ALONG THE EDGES

Continue to squeeze the Dye-Na-Flow in rows from the top to the bottom of the scarf. Spray more water on the scarf.

③ FILL IN GAPS WITH GOLDEN YELLOW

Squeeze Golden Yellow Dye-Na-Flow in between the cool colors you've just applied.

④ SPRINKLE ON SALT

Sprinkle salt onto the scarf. Let the scarf dry. The salt will pull the dye into interesting patterns.

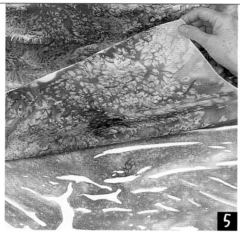

⑤ REMOVE THE SALT AND LIFT OFF THE SCARF

When the scarf is completely dry, brush off the salt and save it to use for your next project. After you have removed the salt, lift the scarf from the illustration board. If you wish, you can frame the printed board as a piece of artwork!

⑥ PLACE TAPE STRIPS OVER ONE CORNER

Tear masking tape into three long strips and several small pieces. Apply them to one corner of the scarf as shown here.

⑦ GLAZE WITH PERIWINKLE

Use a sponge to apply Periwinkle Textile Color over and between selected masked areas. Glazing Textile Color over previously painted or rubber stamped areas adds beautiful depth and dimension to your work.

⑧ GLAZE WITH TURQUOISE

Use a sponge to apply Turquoise Textile Color to additional masked areas.

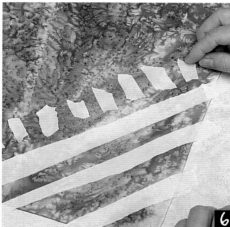

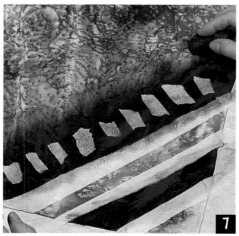

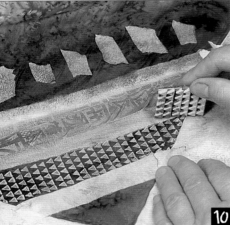

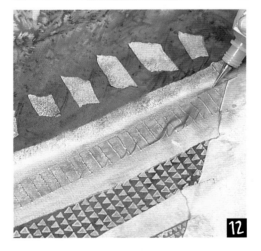

9 ADD BRONZE HIGHLIGHTS

Apply Bronze Lumiere to an uninked stamp pad and use it to ink a Rollagraph stamp wheel. Roll the stamp pattern over one of the Turquoise-glazed areas of the scarf.

10 PRINT PATTERNS IN MINT

Sponge Mint Sorbet onto a rubber stamp. Stamp over one of the Periwinkle-glazed areas.

11 STAMP THE TIP OF THE SCARF

Apply Bronze to a rubber stamp. Stamp the pattern on the bottom triangle of the scarf.

12 ADD MORE BRONZE HIGHLIGHTS

At this point, I looked at the area where I had used the Rollagraph and decided to sponge the entire area with Bronze, letting some of the Rollagraph designs show through. Add a pattern of fine lines on top with Bronze and a 7mm metal applicator tip.

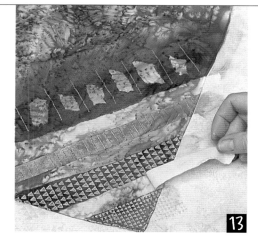

⑬ REMOVE THE TAPE

Add more applicator-tipped lines to selected areas. Pull the masking tape off of the scarf.

➡

The Finished Scarf

The glazes made with Textile Color unify this design while still showing the texture of the salt patterns underneath them. The gold stripes add brilliant accents to the entire piece.

SCARVES FOR EVERY SEASON

These silk scarves are so quick and easy to make that you will want to experiment with a variety of color schemes, perhaps one for every season.

C reating a beautifully decorated surface with stamps and paint is only the beginning. Often the best finishing touches are added to a project long after the paint has dried. Don't be afraid to embellish your work with every imaginable item, such as beads, buttons, collage, charms or ribbons. To me, "more is more." I like rich, textured surfaces. Here are a number of inspirational ways to expand your creativity with embellishments.

Layer Color With Vellum

This simple stapled booklet has a stamped sheet of Sheer Heaven vellum overlaying the cover. The translucency of the vellum creates an extra layer of depth by allowing some of the contrasting colors and patterns underneath to show through. Shrink plastic charms add a nice finishing touch.

Accent Your Piece With a Wood Trim

This fabric collage is a simple yet elegant variation of the Serendipity Wall Hanging on page 105. Glue the top front edge of your collage to the recessed section of a piece of wood molding. You can purchase wood molding from a home improvement store. Then nail a picture hanger onto the back. The wood trim gives you an extra surface to stamp and embellish.

Add Texture With Embossed Metal

The textured stamping on this wood box is beautifully highlighted with medallions made of copper foil. An embossing stylus was used to create the deep ridges and stippled lines in the medallions before gluing them into place. By repeating the pattern made by the stamps in the gel medium, I unified the whole design.

Embellish With Machine Stitching

You can create a fabric collage quickly by simply gluing the pieces onto each other. For a more interesting effect, try stitching the pieces of fabric onto your collage. This collage uses both hand stitching in embroidery floss and machine stitching in finer thread. Both complement nicely the soft, glazed layers of color around them.

➤→

Recycle Found Objects

Occasionally the best embellishments
are the ones you find by accident. That's
the case with the plastic lizard on this
soft-sculpture necklace. Painted a metallic purple and tied down with beads, it
looks perfect alongside the rubber
stamped doll and Tyvek bead. What do
you have on hand that would make a
nice addition to one of your projects?

←◀

Try a Torn Paper Collage

When placed in just the right
spot, torn scraps of stamped
paper can make all the difference in a design. I started this
piece with a background of soft
washes and spattered color from
watercolor crayons. For extra
impact, stamped scraps of paper
were added to frame the central
part of the design with deeper
colors, bolder patterns and
added texture.

➡→

Embellish the Ordinary

Little black handbags sold at discount chain stores make incredibly fun surfaces to stamp and embellish. Bright red-orange and gold charms made of shrink plastic give this whimsical bag an even more playful look. Decorating the zipper pull or flaps is another way to turn a basic black purse into something extraordinary.

◄◄

Highlight Your Favorite Motifs

This piece almost tells a story with its bold use of figures and symbols—day and night, sun and moon. Highlighting the central images with applicator-tipped lines of contrasting color makes it even more dramatic. Choose your own personal motifs and use them to embellish your work.

RESOURCES

Most of the tools and supplies used in this book are readily available at your local craft and art supply stores. You may also find materials by contacting the retailers and manufacturers listed below. Check their Web sites for the store location nearest you.

RETAIL SUPPLIERS IN THE U.S.

A.C. Moore: www.acmoore.com
Hobby Lobby: www.hobbylobby.com
JoAnn Fabrics & Crafts, JoAnn Etc.:
www.joanns.com
Michaels: www.michaels.com
Pearl Paint: www.pearlpaint.com

RETAIL SUPPLIERS IN CANADA

Arts & Crafts Canada:
     www.artsandcraftscanada.com
Craft Canada: www.craftcanada.com

MacPherson Craft Supplies (crafts)
Tel: (519) 284-1741; (800) 238-6663
Web site: www.macphersoncrafts.com

RETAIL SUPPLIERS IN THE UK

Telephone for a store near you.

Craft World
Tel: 07000 757070

Hobby Craft
Tel: 0800 0272387
Web site: www.hobbycraft.co.uk

Katy's Corner
24 St David's Close, Rainhill, Prescot,
Merseyside, L35 4NY
Tel: 0151 431 1835
Web site: www.katyscorner.org.uk
Sheer Heaven vellum

For a good list of rubber stamp stores
75in the UK, visit the Web site:
www.art-e-zine.co.uk/artemalluk.html

MANUFACTURERS

The Adhesive Products, Inc.
520 Cleveland Avenue

Albany, CA 94710
Tel: (510) 526-7616
Web site: www.crafterspick.com
*Crafter's Pick glues: The Ultimate,
Memory Mount, Fabric Glue*

Adica Pongo/Battat, Inc.
P.O. Box 1264
Plattsburgh, NY 12901-0149
Tel: (518) 562-2200; (800) 247-6144
Fax: (518) 562-2203
Das terra cotta air-dry clay

Clearsnap, Inc.
P.O. Box 98
Anacortes, WA 98221
Tel: (888) 448-4862
Web site: www.clearsnap.com
*Stamp pads, Rollagraphs,
Penscore, reinkers*

Cre8it
A division of Gallery Different
8 Chapala Road
Santa Fe, NM 87505
Tel: (505) 466-0270
Web site: www.cre8it.com
*Sheer Heaven vellum, Lamp-In-A-Bag
luminaria kit with shade and
acrylic base lamp*

Golden Artist Colors, Inc.
188 Bell Road
New Berlin, NY 13411-9527
Tel: (800) 959-6543
Web site: www.goldenpaints.com
*Molding pastes, acrylics,
painting mediums*

"Impress Me" Rubber Stamp Company
17116 Escalon Drive

Encino, CA 91436-4030
Tel/Fax: (818) 788-6730
Web site: www.impressmenow.com
Catalog: $5, refundable with a coupon
*Rubber stamps, Sherrill Kahn's Travel
Paint Studio, books by Sherrill Kahn*

Jacquard
Rupert, Gibbon and Spider, Inc.
P.O. Box 425
Healdsburg, CA 95448
Tel: (800) 442-0455
Web site: www.jacquardproducts.com
*Sherrill Kahn's Travel Paint Studio,
Neopaque, Lumiere, Sherrill's Sorbets,
Dye-Na-Flow, Textile Colors, plastic
squeeze bottles and metal applicator
tips, silk scarves*

Kretzer Scissors, Inc.
2787 Margaret Mitchell Drive, NW
Atlanta, GA 30327
Tel: (404) 978-0062
Web site: www.kretzer-scissors.com
Scissors

Lucky Squirrel
P.O. Box 606
Belen, NM 87002
Tel: (800) 462-4912
Web site: www.luckysquirrel.com
PolyShrink shrink plastic

Ranger Industries
15 Park Road
Tinton Falls, NJ 07724
Tel: (800) 244-2211
Web site: www.rangerink.com
*Heatit Craft Tool, stamp pads,
stamping and painting accessories,
Cut n' Dry products, brayers*

CREATE EXTRAORDINARY ART WITH  RUBBER STAMPS

and more!

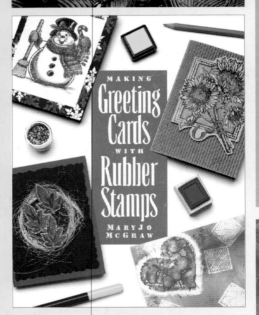

30 MINUTE RUBBER STAMP WORKSHOP

Let Sandra McCall show you how to make gorgeous rubber stamp treasures in 30 minutes or less. From home décor and party favors to desk accessories and wearable gifts, you'll find 27 exciting projects inside. Each one is easy to do and inexpensive to make—perfect for those days when you want to create something quick!

ISBN 1-58180-271-4, paperback, 128 pages, #32142-K

RUBBER STAMP GIFTS

Create rubber stamp masterpieces perfect for gift-giving any time of year! From jewelry boxes and travel journals to greeting cards and candles, Judy Claxton shows you how to make 15 gorgeous projects using easy-to-find materials and simple techniques, such as embellishing, embossing, direct to paper, paper clay, polymer clay and shrink plastic.

ISBN 1-58180-466-0, paperback, 128 pages, #32723-K

MAKING GREETING CARDS WITH RUBBER STAMPS

Here are hundreds of colorful ideas and techniques for creating one-of-a-kind greetings—from the elegant to the festive to the whimsical—all in a matter of minutes! Try your hand at any of the 30 step-by-step projects inside or take off in your own original direction.

ISBN 0-89134-713-5, paperback, 128 pages, #30821-K

RUBBER STAMP EXTRAVAGANZA

Use rubber stamps to decorate candles, jewelry, purses, book covers, wall hangings and more. 16 step-by-step projects show you how by using creative techniques, surfaces and embellishments, including metal, beads, embossing powder and clay—even shrink plastic!

ISBN 1-58180-128-9, paperback, 128 pages, #31829-K